T0329954

Catch-up and Radical Innovation in Chinese State-Owned Enterprises

Exploring Large Infrastructure Projects

Xielin Liu

University of Chinese Academy of Sciences, China

Xiao Wang

Xi'an Jiaotong-Liverpool University, China

Yimei Hu

Aalborg University, Denmark

Edward Elgar
PUBLISHING

Cheltenham, UK • Northampton, MA, USA

Published by
Edward Elgar Publishing Limited
The Lypiatts
15 Lansdown Road
Cheltenham
Glos GL50 2JA
UK

Edward Elgar Publishing, Inc.
William Pratt House
9 Dewey Court
Northampton
Massachusetts 01060
USA

A catalogue record for this book
is available from the British Library

Library of Congress Control Number: 2020950934

This book is available electronically in the **Elgar**online
Economics subject collection
http://dx.doi.org/10.4337/9781781003824

ISBN 978 1 78100 381 7 (cased)
ISBN 978 1 78100 382 4 (eBook)

Printed and bound in Great Britain by TJ Books Limited, Padstow, Cornwall

Contents

Figures

Tables

About the authors

Xielin Liu is a Professor in the School of Economics and Management and the Director of the Research Center for Innovation and Entrepreneurship at the University of Chinese Academy of Sciences. He was a research fellow at the Chinese Academy of Science and Technology for Development, Ministry of Science and Technology (1996–2006), and a professor at Tsinghua University from 1985 to 2006.

Born on September 25, 1957, Prof. Xielin Liu obtained his Bachelor's degree at Peking University, Master's degree at Chinese Academy of Sciences, and PhD at Tsinghua University. His research areas include innovation management and policy, innovation ecosystem, as well as regional and national innovation system. He has published numerous journal articles in academic journals such as *Research Policy*, *Technovation*, *Journal of Management Studies*, *International Journal of Technology Management*, and *Science and Public Policy*. He has also served as an editor of *Research Policy* and related journals and published a number of books in English, such as *Regional Innovation Index of China: 2017* (Springer, 2018), *Environmental Innovation in China* (WIT, 2012), and *Innovation, Technology Policy and Regional Development* with Tim Turpin (Edward Elgar Publishing, 2003).

Xiao Wang is an Assistant Professor in Innovation and Entrepreneurship at
the International Business School Suzhou (IBSS) of Xi'an Jiaotong-Liverpool
University (XJTLU), after earning his Double-PhD degrees awarded by
University of Chinese Academy of Sciences and University of Groningen.
He is also an Honorary Lecturer in Innovation and Entrepreneurship of the
Management School, University of Liverpool, and a Fellow of the Higher
Education Academy (UK). He serves as an article reviewer for several
influential academic journals, such as *Strategic Entrepreneurship Journal,
Human Resource Management* and *Asia Pacific Journal of Management*. Dr.
Dr. Wang also is an Outstanding Teacher of XJTLU, Executive Education
Program Developer and Director (IBSS), Innovation and Entrepreneurship
Mentor of International Innovation Hub (XJTLU), and Research Fellow of
XIPU Institution (think-tank of XJTLU). His research areas include ecosys-
tems of innovation and entrepreneurship, governmental entrepreneurship,
social and knowledge network, and cultural impacts on innovation and entrepreneurship. Besides academic output in journals, such as *Technovation, R&D
Management, Industry and Innovation, Technological Forecasting and Social
Change*, and *Scientometrics*, Dr. Dr. Wang has played a key role in several
think-tank and advisory projects of XJTLU and works as a trainer and advisor
of transcultural collaboration, innovation, and entrepreneurship for enterprises
and governmental agencies.

Yimei Hu is an Associate Professor of Innovation Management in the Business School, Aalborg University, Denmark. She earned her Bachelor's and Master's degrees from Tsinghua University, and her PhD in Business Economics from Aalborg University. Yimei Hu's research interests are innovation and strategic management, focusing on innovation ecosystems, value creation and value capture, and multinational corporations' innovation management. She has won several best paper awards in academic journals and international conferences, and she has published in journals such as *International Journal of Technology Management, European Journal of Innovation Management, European Journal of International Management*, among others. She has also served as a reviewer for leading international innovation journals, such as *Management and Organization Review, IEEE Transactions on Engineering Management, International Journal of Technology Management, European Journal of Innovation Management, Innovation: Management and Organization*, and others. In addition to her academic research contributions, Yimei Hu has been an active lecturer in various international study programs, such as that of the Sino-Danish Centre for Education and Research, and also serves as a consultancy expert for think-tanks such as BISTI and industrial associations such as IOGEI in Hong Kong.

Preface[1]

There have been many books on China's rise, and the country's innovation over 40 years from 1978 to 2019. Economists tend to explain the rise of China from the perspectives of joining the World Trade Organization (WTO) and benefiting from the demographic dividend of low labor costs. Political scholars interpret China's success as being due to its state capitalism regime. Academic researchers in science and technological innovations strive to explore a Chinese model of innovation that is distinct from the Western one.

In this book, we focus on state-owned enterprises (SOEs), the backbone of the Chinese economy, and investigate how the large SOEs make radical innovation in their respective industries possible. Some may argue that SOEs are simply relying on governmental subsidies. If that is true, then could SOEs' innovation be sustainable?

This books focuses on SOEs' innovation in four industries and shows how Chinese SOEs, as key players in radical innovation, have transformed the industrial infrastructure of China, from lagging far behind to becoming a global leader; and how Chinese SOEs have changed their role in the global competition landscape, from followers and imitators to world-leading innovators.

We propose that the catch-up and rise of Chinese SOEs' innovation reveal a new kind of approach: with the advantage of political support, they undertake innovation by utilizing or building a relevant ecosystem. In their respective industries, they quite often play the role of lead users to guide the complex innovation processes. They take advantage of the windows of opportunity to enter the innovation war in the industries. Therefore, this book highlights how – based on the user-centered innovation ecosystem – Chinese SOEs are achieving victory in the innovation war.

This book is the result of a long academic journey. We initially planned to tell the stories of both SOEs and private enterprises in one book. However, we encountered substantial challenges. Eventually, we decided to leave our exploration of innovation in private enterprises for a later book. We also planned to find a good framework for explaining and understanding Chinese

[1] This book is an outcome of the project supported by the National Natural Science Foundation of China: No.71932009; IFREM Alliance Program; and IBSS Development Fund.

SOEs' radical innovation. After research and discussion, we concluded that the user-centered innovation ecosystem fits our cases very well. We consider the SOEs' innovations included in this book to be radical innovations because they have an immense impact on various sectors in China.

We thank the China Enterprise Confederation for helping us to arrange the research visits to those large SOEs from 2015 to 2017. Also a sincere thank-you to China General Nuclear Power Corporation, State Grid, China Mobile, and China South Locomotive & Rolling Stock, regarding their great support to our field researchers.

The research on radical innovation in China is a result of our ongoing academic efforts. Many of our former and current students contributed greatly to this book. We thank: Jian Chen, Researcher at the Chinese Research Academy of S&T for Development; Peng Cheng, Associate Professor at Beijing Forest University; Xuemei Ma, Researcher at China Aerospace Engineering Science and Technology Development Strategy Research Institute, Beijing; Yuchen Gao, Postdoctoral Researcher at Tsinghua University; and Xi Wang, Peipei Yang, Xuechen Ding, and Caiting Dong, doctoral candidates at the School of Economics and Management, University of Chinese Academy of Sciences.

We also appreciate the following contributors from Xi'an Jiaotong-Liverpool University: Jianing Dong, Yuan Gao, Yujie Han, Yicong Mei, Yang Nan, Lujie Wang, Sirui Wang, Yiyang Wang, and Tianyu Xiang.

A sincere thank-you also goes to Xinzhi Chang from University of Chinese Academy of Sciences, who contributed to Chapter 2.

Xielin Liu, Xiao Wang, and Yimei Hu
December 5, 2020

1. State-owned enterprise, government, and the innovation ecosystem

1.1 INTRODUCTION

Innovation has been considered the source of economic growth and national competitiveness since Schumpeter's pioneering work in 1912. Nowadays, governments in both developed and developing countries are putting more and more emphasis on innovation as their top agenda.

For many years, the planned economy was criticized for its inefficiency in resource allocation and lack of incentives for entrepreneurship and innovation. As a result, few radical innovations stemmed from the (former) Soviet Union or China between the 1950s and 1970s.

Since 1978, China has been on a long journey of transition from a pure socialist economy to a socialist market economy. After 40 years of transition, China has become the second-largest economy in the world, with rapid progress in science, technology, and innovation. As Figure 1.1 shows, China sustained 37 years of rapid gross domestic product (GDP) growth from 1981 through 2017. Compared with other countries, China's economic development has been growing fast in recent years, and the country has gradually become a leader in the world economy.

As shown in Figure 1.2, in 1991, China's research and development (R&D) investment (gross expenditure on R&D, GERD) accounted for a smaller proportion of its GDP compared with other countries, whereas from 2007 to 2017, the percentage of its R&D investment increased and approached that of other countries. This indicates that China gradually realized that investment in science and technology would be the key to promoting economic development and technological progress.

In terms of the number of patents, which is an indicator of innovation capability, China has been catching up rapidly. This is apparent from an international comparison using the number of patents granted in the United States (US). Table 1.1 shows that the number of patents granted by the US to Chinese enterprises has increased dramatically since 2005, though that number still lags behind that of developed countries. The rise in the number of US patents

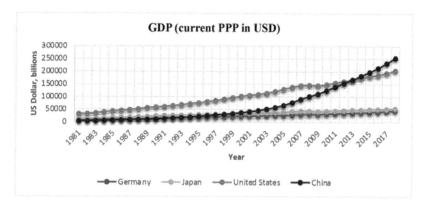

Figure 1.1   *GDP of Germany, Japan, the US, and China from 1981 to 2017*

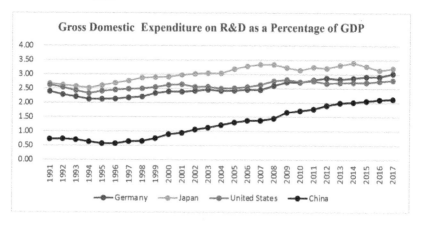

Figure 1.2   *GERD of Germany, Japan, the US, and China*

granted to Chinese firms implies that new technologies are emerging and flourishing in China's technology markets.

There are many different explanations for the rise of China in the last 40 years. One well-cited explanation is that China is a country of state capitalism (Bremmer, 2010). Ian Bremmer (2009b), in "State capitalism comes of age: The end of the free market?", a widely circulated article published in *Foreign Affairs*, argues that the 2008 financial crisis exposed the Achilles heel of the free market system and suggested that state capitalism was the correct antidote to the excesses of capitalism. In this article, as well as in his book, *The End of the Free Market: Who Wins the War between States and Corporations?*

Table 1.1   *Number of patents granted by the US Patent and Trademark Office (USPTO) to international corporate applicants*

Year	China	Brazil	India	Russia	South Africa	Germany	Japan	Republic of Korea
1995	62	63	37	98	123	6 600	21 764	1 161
2000	119	98	131	183	111	10 234	31 296	3 314
2005	402	77	384	148	87	9 011	30 341	4 352
2010	2 657	175	1 098	272	116	12 363	44 814	11 671
2014	7 236	334	2 987	445	152	16 550	53 849	16 469
Annual growth rate in different periods (%)								
1995–2005	21	2	26	4	-3	3	3	14
2005–2014	38	18	26	13	6	7	7	16
1995–2014	28	9	26	8	1	5	5	15

Source: Computed by authors, based on data from the USPTO.

(Bremmer, 2010), Bremmer goes further and argues that state capitalism is not just an anti-cyclical tool, but also a source of China's long-run economic boom. Yet Yasheng Huang argues that, while state capitalism is a source of success, it also triggers many structural problems in today's Chinese economy, such as its unsustainable high level of investment; its massive and, most likely, increasingly unproductive accumulation of debt; and the lackluster growth of labor income compared to GDP growth (Huang, 2008).

Some have pointed out that the Chinese story is a result of globalization, especially after China joined the WTO in 1999, when a great number of advanced technologies and a great deal of information and knowledge began to flow into China. Baldwin (2016) explains that China's rise in terms of efficiency was based on the combination of Western know-how and Chinese low labor costs, which triggered the Chinese "manufacturing miracle."

As we stated in the Preface, our intention in this book is to explain the rise of China's economy from the angle of large state-owned enterprises (SOEs), a group of companies that researchers tend to regard as less efficient and less capable of innovation than private enterprises as a result of the agency problem. It is true that before the economic and market reform of 1978, SOEs dominated the Chinese economy as the only legitimate economic institution in China. Since 1978, SOEs have gone through a series of reforms, which will be elaborated upon in detail later in this book. The truth is that, after the reform, SOEs in China did not disappear from the landscape of economic competition. On the contrary, they are still powerful, especially in the infrastructure sector. Indeed, some large SOEs are now the leading companies in their respective industries.

There have been a great number of studies on whether Chinese SOEs can innovate. One argument is that, given the unclear property rights of large SOEs, they are in a state of no ownership; thus, SOEs' leaders probably lack the motivation to innovate to make more profit (Zhou et al., 2017). Another view is that SOEs are bureaucratic, and their overstaffed organizational structures are unable to respond to market changes rapidly. Hence, SOEs can carry out only incremental innovation instead of breakthrough innovation (Yip and McKern, 2016). The third viewpoint is that since all SOE leaders are appointed for a five-year term, this prevents them from developing long-term strategies and investing in risky innovation projects (Peng et al., 2004). Moreover, many criticize SOEs for lacking innovation: enjoying substantial protection from foreign competition, SOEs can gain profits from completely monopolistic positions in a number of core industries (Zhu, 2012; Branstetter and Feenstra, 2002; Amiti and Smarzynska, 2008), hence they do not need to innovate.

Though there are so many limitations on SOEs innovating, in fact, there have been very successful cases of SOE innovations, such as the high-speed train, ultra-high voltage power transmission, and 4G telecommunications. So, the question is why those SOEs are so innovative. Some argue that China's whole-nation system plays a dominant role[1] in pooling nationwide resources to help address the country's major challenges, and thus achieve significant breakthroughs in technologies at a relatively fast pace. Indeed, by virtue of this whole-nation system, a number of successes were achieved, such as the atomic and hydrogen bombs and artificial satellite projects in the 1960s and 1970s, and the space flight and lunar exploration projects started in the 2000s. Besides the whole-nation system, the SOEs were also conducive to the recent remarkable radical innovations being discussed in this book.

Instead of understanding innovation in Chinese SOEs from the perspectives of ownership structure, monopolistic position, administration, and so on, a new approach is adopted by this book: the innovation ecosystem. Our main argument is that, in the transitional period, many large SOEs have successfully leveraged the advantages of both the planned economy and the market mechanism to innovate in some large infrastructure projects. They have done so by using the ecosystem approach to mobilize and coordinate the resources needed for these complex projects.

---

[1]   http://www.sasac.gov.cn/n2588025/n4423279/n4517386/n9281016/c9310465/content.html.

1.2   INNOVATION ECOSYSTEM

Both the concept and the theoretical approach of the innovation ecosystem have emerged in recent years and become popularized in the management literature. The attractiveness of the concept is based, first, on the understanding that innovation is a critical driver of firms' long-term growth and sustained competitive advantage (Ahuja and Lampert, 2001). Second, the ecosystem view highlights the fact that the complexity level of innovation is increasing; this is seen in the interdependent and complementary relationships between related ecosystem partners, such as suppliers, users and complementors, and the relationships have become increasingly important for firms to successfully innovate (Adner, 2006; Adner and Kapoor, 2010; Dyer and Singh, 1998; Dyer et al., 2018).

The term "ecosystem," borrowed from biology, is viewed as "the collaborative arrangements through which firms combine their individual offerings into a coherent, customer-facing solution" (Adner, 2006). An innovation ecosystem consists of a focal firm, its upstream suppliers, and its downstream customers and complementors (Adner and Kapoor, 2010). The innovation ecosystem describes the interdependent relationships among various actors of innovation and technologies, emphasizing their modularity and complementarities (Jacobides et al., 2018; Moore, 1996).

From the innovation ecosystem perspective, for a focal firm's innovation or focal value proposition to be successful it must be accompanied by the technological advancement and actions of its complementors in the ecosystem (Adner and Kapoor, 2010; Jacobides et al., 2018). The realization of a focal value proposition is influenced by various aspects of complementarities, such as the key components relying on interdependent technologies delivered by suppliers, the supportive production or infrastructure for an innovation provided by actors from adjacent industries, and the demand created by customers (Adner, 2017; Moore, 1996).

Nowadays, no enterprise is capable of carrying out all of the innovation activities in a certain sector; indeed, even on the national level, no nation state is equipped with the full range of industries. Thus, innovation is gradually becoming a joint effort of business actors across companies, industries, and national boundaries. Associated with such a trend, the innovation competition between businesses and nations has gradually become a competition among ecosystems (Adner, 2006; Adner and Kapoor, 2010). As a result of such development of business ecosystems, especially in the context of global innovation, the era of the innovation ecosystem has begun.

In 1993, Moore put forward the term "business ecosystem," with the belief that a company should be viewed as part of a business ecosystem covering a variety of industries (Moore, 1993). In a business ecosystem, companies work both cooperatively and competitively to support new products, satisfy customer needs, and eventually form a structured community. Every business ecosystem evolves through four distinct stages: birth, expansion, leadership, and self-renewal (Moore, 1993). In addition, actors in a business ecosystem make conscious choices by understanding the situation at hand and contemplating outcomes (Moore, 1996).

Although there exist divergent definitions of the innovation ecosystem, we believe that it can be seen as a form of the business ecosystem. One may regard it as an organizational system with innovative elements – including technology, talent, market, operation mode, and culture – that form a coherent and customer-oriented solution (Adner, 2006). The innovation ecosystem is also widely regarded as a network that consists of core enterprises or platforms, suppliers, and customers, and that creates and utilizes new values with innovation (Autio and Thomas, 2014). Recently, its network-based reach has further expanded: besides the aforementioned components, users, governments, universities and scientific research institutions, intermediaries, venture capitalists, and other relevant social entities are now included. All of these entities jointly constitute a number of complementary and cooperative networks (Liu et al., 2016).

SOEs in general have some unique features that other organizations do not, such as the significant role of government, complementors inherited from the former planned economy, and their strategic and leading position in their respective industries. The next section looks more closely at SOEs' innovation ecosystem.

1.3   SOES' INNOVATION ECOSYSTEM

SOEs in China have developed their particular innovation ecosystems in order to survive and grow. These ecosystems have the following features.

First, due to the resource advantages and strategic role of SOEs in China, they mainly undertake state-level projects of great complexity, such as the innovations of high-speed rail and 4G mobile telecommunications. Thus, in such an innovation ecosystem, there is usually a rather influential corporation with support from the government. The corporation acts as the leader and mobilizer in its industry and can be a manufacturer, a platform, or a contractor having specific technical capabilities, as well as upstream and downstream business partners.

Second, due to the particular role of SOEs, their innovations are more related to generic technologies (GTs) which have significant complementarity with existing or potential new technologies (Moser and Nicholas, 2004). The exploitation of these technologies will yield benefits for a wide range of sectors of the economy and/or society (Martin, 1993), such as promoting the entire industry's and even peripheral industries' development. Successfully developing GTs relies on actors who work on technologies and markets (Kokshagina et al., 2017), on basic research programs (Novelli, 2010), as well as on further developed, comprehensive systems (Rosenberg, 1976). Thus, the innovation ecosystems of Chinese SOEs usually are quite complex and inclusive in terms of the components and the value chain.

Third, both traditional and newer-generation coordination mechanisms are used in the ecosystems of Chinese SOEs. Traditionally, the SOEs did not have much market freedom due to government control (Park et al., 2006), despite having wholly owned upstream and downstream subsidiaries. However, after the reform, the traditional industrial chains broke down or collapsed, such as those of the SOEs directly affiliated with the (former) Ministry of Electric Power Industry, the Ministry of Water Resources, and the (former) Ministry of Railways. Following the reform of those governmental departments and affiliated SOEs, the players in the industrial chains changed significantly, and the prior collaborations among business partners directed by the government decreased, whereas spontaneous partnerships for mutual business development against external competition increased. Thus, the current business networks of SOEs are more diverse: more universities, public research institutes, and banks are involved in the SOEs' ecosystems for sustainability, while the government continues to play a supplementary role, such as providing policies, funding, and infrastructure to catalyze the innovation ecosystems' autonomy and openness. However, for the projects that have strategic implications for GT development, the traditional government-led coordination mechanism in the innovation ecosystems still plays a critical role, which greatly increases the efficiency of coordination, resource allocation, and collaboration.

Fourth, to a great extent, the innovation ecosystems developed by SOEs are open systems that stemmed from the early decades of China's reform and opening-up of the economy. When China started to attract foreign direct investment (FDI) early on, the SOEs became the first candidates for joint ventures. Today, in China's automobile industry, most of the largest joint ventures partner with large SOEs. With the economic development of China, Chinese SOEs also conduct outward FDI activities, with significant influence in some industries across the world (Cui and Jiang, 2012; Morck et al., 2008). SOEs are becoming new and significant players in global markets and are now more likely to invest abroad (Duanmu, 2014). The *China Statistical Yearbook 2013–2017* (National Bureau of Statistics of China, 2014–2018) provides details on the income of SOEs that are cooperating with foreign enterprises, as shown in Figure 1.3.

Overall, the SOE's innovation ecosystems are based on huge market demand in China and on well-coordinated supply systems, with the participation of

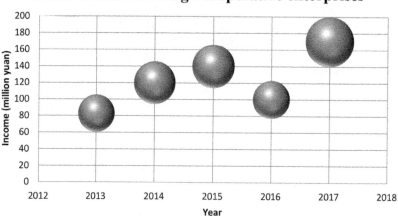

Figure 1.3   *Income of SOEs cooperating with foreign enterprises in 2013–2017*

universities, research institutions, financing institutions and the government. As part of their evolution, SOEs are collaborating more with global partners to advance technology and create joint market development. With the government's strategies aimed at incorporating world trends into China's long-term development, the outcomes of the SOEs' innovation ecosystems, such as new products and technologies, are creating considerable value for end-users.

1.4   THE CHINESE GOVERNMENT'S ROLES IN SOES' INNOVATION ECOSYSTEMS

When talking about the special ecosystems developed around Chinese SOEs, the role of government cannot be neglected. In fact, some refer to the Chinese mode of innovation as the state-led innovation system (Bremmer, 2009a).

Innovation stems from market competition and entrepreneurship (Schumpeter, 1934). In the US, the free market is regarded as the best system for allocating innovation resources. Any governmental action would distort market operations (Bremmer, 2010) or, as 18th-century British economist Adam Smith called it, the "invisible hand." In a free market, private enterprises are the main actors in an innovation system. Government intervention works only in areas where the market fails, and government is thus either distrusted or operating at a low level of intervention.

However, this indicates that the "visible hand," namely the nation or state, can play a very important role in a country's competitiveness. This principle has been widely adopted in developing or catching-up countries, where the most successful companies are chosen as the main actors in helping the nation to accomplish its developmental strategies. An important point is that the enterprises in developing countries, versus those in developed countries, tend to be weak in terms of innovation capabilities and resources. Therefore, in this "catching-up" stage, the representative East Asian countries' governments used industrial policy to support their enterprises: for example, the technological and economic rise of Japan, Korea, and Singapore was in each case, to some extent, due to governmental intervention in industrial development (Freeman, 1989; Okimoto, 1989).

The Chinese economy is neither a coordinated market economy nor a liberal market economy; its institutional context is quite different from that of the Western economies. The government plays a rather substantial role in recognizing long-term market opportunities which have profound implications for national development and economic rejuvenation, as well as for facilitating joint exploitation of those opportunities by enterprises. As innovation leads to economic growth and catch-up, the country's primary goal – promoting innovation – becomes a critical concern. The Chinese government deploys three main tools to promote innovation: the national science and technology (S&T) strategy and program, the industrial policy, and the industrial regulation.

Strategy Setting

As a developing country, China has persistently used the strategy of technological innovation to empower the nation. The Chinese higher education system largely stagnated during the Cultural Revolution from 1966 to 1976, and higher education enrollment was also stopped. Deng Xiaoping, in 1978, said that science and technology are the primary productive forces. He initiated the first national high-tech program, called "863," and restored the higher education system and the science and technology system in 1977, so that many scientists could return to their work in laboratories. In 1995, Jiang Zemin's administration initiated the strategy of "science and education for a prosperous China," as well as innovation programs at Chinese Academy of Sciences (CAS), and the strategy of informatization as a parallel wave of industrialization of China. In the next administration, Hu Jintao set up a new goal for China – to be an innovative country by 2020 – and proposed the indigenous innovation strategy. Furthering the previous leadership's spirit, the current president, Xi Jinping, has established an additional strategy, "innovation-driven development," which is regarded as the new engine for China's sustainable economic and social development.

A typical example of the current strategy was the enactment of the latest National Medium- and Long-term Plan for Development of Science and Technology (MLPST) (2006–2020) in 2006. The goal of this national program was to make China an innovative country by implementing an indigenous innovation strategy. The specific goals were to increase the proportion of R&D expenditures in GDP to 2 percent by 2010 and to 2.5 percent by 2020; to make science and technology and innovation the most important enabling factors for GDP growth, contributing about 60 percent of GDP growth; to reduce the dependence on foreign technology to less than 30 percent (the ratio of expenditures on technology imports to R&D expenditures was estimated at 56 percent in 2004); and, finally, to be among the top five countries worldwide in terms of the number of domestic invention patents granted and the number of international citations of scientific papers (State Council of China, 2006).

By following this strategy, China has continuously increased R&D expenditures, even during the financial crisis of 2008, whereas some developed countries stagnated or reduced their R&D and education investment. In 2010, China's ratio of R&D to GDP reached 1.76 percent, up from 0.6 percent in 1996. Therefore, many reports and research papers (e.g., Chesbrough, 2010; Sigurdson, 2004) have considered China to be the next science, technology, and innovation superpower.

The MLPST has made huge impacts on the development of industries and technological innovation. With the strategy of indigenous innovation and building an innovative country, China launched 16 mega-projects to upgrade the corporate innovation capabilities in key industries. These projects accelerated the national R&D investment, which would reach 2.5 percent by 2020. Focusing on enhancing the technological capabilities of industries with particular strategic importance, Councillor Liu Yandong further called for the establishment of a robust market economy based on the new nationwide resource-pooling system (the whole-nation system) (Liu, 2008).

Industrial Policy and S&T Subsidies

Some research has suggested that Japanese industrial policy and the Ministry of International Trade and Industry (MITI) greatly helped Japanese companies to catch up, and drove Japan's economic growth (Johnson, 1982). Similarly, industrial policy has played a critical role in China. In 1978, Deng Xiaoping proposed that science and technology were the primary productive forces. From 1986 to 1997, the central government launched and financially supported several key S&T programs, such as 863 (high-tech), 973 (basic research projects with national strategic importance), and the Torch and Star Program. The idea was that the government would intervene in science and technology processes for the national interest. In each five-year plan, several industries with strategic importance for the sustainable development and global competitiveness of China would be selected as key or strategic industries. Those industries would get more favorable support, such as land, capital, and tax reductions.

China's central government has been supporting high-tech industries for many years, but in more recent years, strategic emerging industries have become the focus, attracting R&D subsidies, public procurement, and favorable bank loans. Along with the S&T development in China, establishing industrial standards and initiating mega-projects have become more advanced policy tools to promote innovation. Take the Twelfth Five-Year Plan, which began in 2012, as an example: the Chinese government selected 16 mega-projects to promote national innovation in key strategic industries, such as general-purpose central processing units (CPUs), large commercial aircraft, next-generation telecommunications technology, nuclear power plants, new drugs, and lunar landing. All of these mega-projects have been entrusted to the leading SOEs (Lu et al., 2012). Moreover, to facilitate the national innovation strategy and to mitigate the uncertainties associated with innovation projects, the Chinese government has begun to deploy new tax policies to subsidize firms with heavy R&D investment.

Regulation

As China is vast in territory and population, divergent in market attributes and segments, and underdeveloped in its institutions and market system, Chinese enterprises are usually weak and myopic in technological development and innovation. Thus, government intervention is necessary to reduce market failures and to protect the national interest. The regulation of industrial development and innovation is thus an effective policy tool.

Government departments and agencies enact various regulations to facilitate innovation in different ways. Among them, the National Development and Reform Commission (NDRC) is the most powerful national agency that regulates industries in terms of investment scale, scope, and volume. The Ministry of Industry and Information Technology (MIIT) plays a similar role in the industry of information technology (IT). For instance, in the 1990s, analyzing the competition between the WCDMA and CDMA2000 networks, MIIT promoted TD-SCDMA as the national standard to compete with the other two 3G standards and involved two SOEs, Datang and China Mobile, as the key players. In addition, the Ministry of Science and Technology (MOST) plays an essential role in regulating the development of science and technology, as well as in guiding the activities and organizations of science and technology to foster S&T development in industries (Pearson et al., 2012).

Other Subsidies

In addition to the government's science and technology subsidy, the national financial and banking system also plays an irreplaceable role in financing SOEs' innovation, development and growth. Apart from being encouraged by local officials to set up "stabilization loans" to SOEs (Cull and Xu, 2003), both national commercial banks and private banks are encouraged by the central and local governments to provide loans to SOEs (Eckaus, 2006). Also, since local governments often have both managerial and fiduciary authority over the SOEs operating locally, they can provide them with direct subsidies (Eckaus, 2006). As SOEs are usually delegated to accomplish the national "developmental missions," including leading the national technological advancement, the central government provides more financial support, as evidenced by the recent sharp growth of state-level Industrial Guidance Funds.

1.5   RADICAL INNOVATION IN THE LARGE INFRASTRUCTURE SECTOR

The focus of this book is innovation in different industries of the large infrastructure sector, such as high-speed railway, nuclear power plants, super-high voltage electricity, and 4G telecommunications. These innovation projects need large investments over a long time span and, more importantly, the support of considerable stakeholders. Further, the above-mentioned innovation projects are very complex, with iterative stages from R&D, to engineering, to deployment and service. They also have large spillover effects for the respective industries and markets. Therefore, considering the complexity, enormous investments, and public goods attributes of such innovation projects, only large SOEs have the capabilities and legitimacy to lead the way.

Radical innovation usually incorporates completely new and highly complex technologies and, in the process, reshapes the market structure. On the demand side, these innovations induce significant behavior changes of users, who have to learn to use the new technologies (e.g., Urban et al., 1996). It is true that in China, innovation is incremental, more often than not, and the most astonishing innovations usually involve business models, such as the model underlying Alibaba's e-commerce empire. Yet, in those industries of the large infrastructure sector, Chinese SOEs have demonstrated to the world that their achievements – in terms of both technology and market – are remarkable and deserve the name of "radical innovation."

REFERENCES

Adner, R. (2006). Match your innovation strategy to your innovation ecosystem. *Harvard Business Review, 84*(4), 98–107, 148.

Adner, R. (2017). Ecosystem as structure: An actional construct for strategy. *Journal of Management, 43*(1), 39–58.

Adner, R., and Kapoor, R. (2010). Value creation in innovation ecosystems: How the structure of technological interdependence affects firm performance in new technology generations. *Strategic Management Journal, 31*(3), 306–333.

Ahuja, G., and Lampert, C.M. (2001). Entrepreneurship in the large corporation: A longitudinal study of how established firms create breakthrough inventions. *Strategic Management Journal, 22*(6–7), 521–543.

Amiti, M., and Smarzynska, J.B. (2008). Trade costs and location of foreign firms in China. *Journal of Development Economics, 85*(1–2), 129–149.

Autio, E., and Thomas, L. (2014). Innovation ecosystem: Implications for innovation management. In M. Dodgson, D.M. Gann, and N. Phillips (eds), *The Oxford Handbook of Innovation Management* (pp. 204–288). Oxford: Oxford University Press.

Baldwin, R. (2016). *The Great Convergence: Information Technology and the New Globalization.* Cambridge, MA: Belknap Press of Harvard University Press.

Branstetter, L.G., and Feenstra, R.C. (2002). Trade and foreign direct investment in China: A political economy approach. *Journal of International Economics, 58*(2), 335–358.

Bremmer, I. (2009a). State capitalism and the crisis. *Mckinsey Quarterly*, July, 1–17.

Bremmer, I. (2009b). State capitalism comes of age: The end of the free market? *Foreign Affairs, 88*(3), 40–56.

Bremmer, I. (2010). *The End of the Free Market: Who Wins the War between States and Corporations?* New York: Portfolio, Penguin Group.

Chesbrough, H. (2010). China, innovation superpower: How to deal with it. November 11, Forbes.

Cui, L., and Jiang F. (2012). State ownership effect on firms' FDI ownership decisions under institutional pressure: A study of Chinese outward-investing firms. *Journal of International Business Studies, 43*(3), 264–284.

Cull, R., and Xu, L.C. (2003). Who gets credit? The behavior of bureaucrats and state banks in allocating credit to Chinese state-owned enterprises. *Journal of Development Economics, 71*(2), 533–559.

Duanmu, J.L. (2014). State-owned MNCs and host country expropriation risk: The role of home state soft power and economic gunboat diplomacy. *Journal of International Business Studies, 45*(8), 1044–1060.

Dyer, J.H., and Singh, H. (1998). The relational view: Cooperative strategy and sources of interorganizational competitive advantage, *Academy of Management Review, 23*, 660–679.

Dyer, J.H., Singh, H., and Hesterly, W.S. (2018). The relational view revisited: A dynamic perspective on value creation and value capture. *Strategic Management Journal, 39*(12), 3140–3162.

Eckaus, R.S. (2006). China's exports, subsidies to state-owned enterprises and the WTO. *China Economic Review, 17*(1), 1–13.

Freeman, C. (1989). *Technology Policy and Economic Performance.* London: Pinter Publishers.

Huang, Y. (2008). *Capitalism with Chinese Characteristics: Entrepreneurship and the State*. Cambridge: Cambridge University Press.

Jacobides, M.G., Cennamo, C., and Gawer, A. (2018). Towards a theory of ecosystems. *Strategic Management Journal*, 39(8), 2255–2276.

Johnson, C. (1982). *MITI and the Japanese Miracle: The Growth of Industrial Policy: 1925–1975*. Stanford, CA: Stanford University Press.

Kokshagina, O., Gillier, T., Cogez, P., Le Masson, P., and Weil, B. (2017). Using innovation contests to promote the development of generic technologies. *Technological Forecasting and Social Change*, 114, 152–164.

Liu, X.L. (2008). *Globalization, Catch-up and Innovation* (in Chinese). Beijing: Science Press.

Liu, X., Ma, X., and Gao, Y. (2016). The strategy of innovation ecosystem on their performances (in Chinese), *Science of Science and S&T Management*, 37(8), 102–115.

Lu, H., Przybyla, A., Reed, L., and Xu, M.W. (2012). A framework and case studies to evaluate China's megaprojects and strategic emerging industries. Working Paper presented at the Conference on the Structure, Process and Leadership of the Chinese Science and Technology System, University of California Institute on Global Conflict and Cooperation.

Martin, B. (1993). *Research Foresight and the Exploitation of the Science Base*. London: HM Stationery Office.

Moore, J.F. (1993). Predators and prey: A new ecology of competition. *Harvard Business Review*, 71(3), 75.

Moore, J.F. (1996). *The Death of Competition: Leadership and Strategy in the Age of Business Ecosystem*. New York: Harper Paperbacks.

Morck, R., Yeung, B., and Zhao, M. (2008). Perspectives on China's outward foreign direct investment. *Journal of International Business Studies*, 39(3), 337–350.

Moser, P., and Nicholas, T. (2004). Was electricity a general purpose technology? Evidence from historical patent citations. *American Economic Review*, 94(2), 388–394.

National Bureau of Statistics of China (2014–2018). *The China Statistical Yearbook 2013–2017*, Beijing: China Statistics Press.

Novelli, E. (2010). As you sow, so shall you reap: General technologies and entry into new product subfields in the face of technological uncertainty. In DRUID Conference, London, June.

Okimoto, D.I. (1989). *Between MITI and the Market: Japanese Industrial Policy for High Technology*. Stanford, CA: Stanford University Press.

Park, S.H., Li, S., and David, K.T. (2006). Market liberalization and firm performance during China's economic transition. *Journal of International Business Studies*, 37(1), 127–147.

Pearson, M., Suttmeier, R.P., and Lin, Z. (2012). The governance of science and technology in China: In search of a framework. Available at SSRN 3285509. In Conference on the Structure, Process, and Leadership of the Chinese Science and Technology System, University of California, San Diego, La Jolla, CA, July 16–17.

Peng, M.W., Tan, J., and Tong, T.M. (2004). Ownership types and strategic groups in an emerging economy. *Journal of Management Studies*, 41(7), 1105–1129.

Rosenberg, N. (1976). *Perspectives on Technology*. Cambridge: Cambridge University Press.

Schumpeter, J.A. (1934). *The Theory of Economic Development*. Cambridge, MA: Harvard University Press.

Sigurdson, J. (2004). Technological superpower China? *R&D Management, 34,* 345–347.

State Council of China (2006). *Some Complementary Policy for National Long and Middle-Range S&T Programming for 2006–2020.* Beijing: State Council of China.

Urban, G.L., Weinberg, B.D., and Hauser, J.R. (1996). Premarket forecasting of really new products. *Journal of Marketing, 60* (1), 47–60.

Yip, G., and McKern, B. (2016). *China's Next Strategic Advantage: From Imitation to Innovation,* Cambridge, MA: MIT Press.

Zhou, K.Z., Gao, G.Y., and Zhao, H. (2017). State ownership and firm innovation in China: An integrated view of institutional and efficiency logics. *Administrative Science Quarterly, 62*(2), 375–404.

Zhu, X. (2012). Understanding China's growth: Past, present, and future. *Journal of Economic Perspectives, 26*(4), 103–124.

2. Formation of the dual innovation systems in China

Xielin Liu, Xiao Wang, Yimei Hu and Xinzhi Chang

Based on the concept of the innovation system, some researchers introduced the term "dual innovation system," which means the simultaneous innovation of a product and a technology to be applied in that product (Brilhuis-Meijer et al., 2016). In China, the government intervenes considerably in some industries, with the purpose of facilitating a catch-up strategy. In other industries, however, the market mechanism or the "invisible hand" plays a more important role, allowing many private enterprises, such as Huawei and Lenovo, to innovate with their own business models.

In China, there are two kinds of innovation systems: the national innovation systems, which consist of major players such as the central government, state-owned enterprises (SOEs), universities and governmental research institutes such as Chinese Academy of Sciences (CAS); and the market-driven innovation systems, which are composed of private enterprises (PEs), regional industrial clusters, and even global business networks. The two kinds of innovation systems can function complementarily (for example, in the telecommunications industry), work separately (for example, more PEs clustered in the wind power and photovoltaic industries, compared to SOEs), or even compete with each other (for example, in the automobile industry). Basically, the market-driven innovation systems operate as most innovation systems all over the world, whereas the national systems are unique, especially in terms of how SOEs innovate and how the other actors interact with the SOEs.

The focus of this book is to share the stories of representative Chinese SOEs' innovations, and scrutinize the key enabling factors and evolutionary processes of those innovations. In this chapter, we adopt the term "dual innovation systems" to explain how this particular institutional arrangement – one with state-owned enterprises and the other with private enterprises as the main actor – determined the disparate motivation, pattern and accessible resource of SOEs' and PEs' innovation, and how in such a system the SOEs and PEs were stimulated to build up their specialties with suitable industry orientations, and collaborate as well as compete with each other.

2.1   EVOLUTION OF SOES' ROLE

Although Chinese private enterprises (PEs) and foreign multinational enterprises play an indispensable role in some industries such as information technology (IT) (for example, Huawei, Lenovo, Nokia, Motorola, Samsung, Ericsson, and AT&T), the powerful influence of large SOEs undertaking and implementing national strategies in other industries can hardly be neglected, such as utilities, infrastructure, oil, and banking. Even in the IT industry, the largest operators of mobile telecommunications are SOEs (China Mobile, China Telecom, and China Unicom). These SOEs are expected to exemplify the value of governmental intervention in technological, economic, and societal development.

Following the example of the former Soviet Union, China deployed the socialist system and a planned economy in 1949. Like other socialist economies, state-owned enterprises used to be the only legal entities conducting economic activities. From 1949 to the 1980s, the SOEs in various industries, such as steel, automobiles, machinery, and railways, only tried to specialize in equipment and component manufacturing under the control of the central or local government (Liu and White, 2001). In 1978, when China initiated its economic reform and opening up, SOEs generated almost 80 percent of the industrial output and provided lifetime employment opportunities; that is, the "iron rice bowl." Nonetheless, the planned economy has been proved to be less efficient than a market economy.

In 1978, the GDP per capita of China was insignificant, only US$57, compared to the United Kingdom (US$5977), Japan (US$8675), and the United States (US$10 600). The main reason for this discrepancy was that Chinese SOEs lacked global competence compared to the PEs in market economies. With the (former) Soviet Union's decline, the appeal for privatization started to be a strong voice with regard to China's economic development and sustainability. In essence, privatization assumes that people are better motivated to develop privately owned ventures and to use resources more efficiently in the context of competitive markets (Majocchi and Strange, 2012; Megginson and Netter, 2001).

In the late 1990s, Premier Zhu Rongji implemented several radical measures to improve the SOEs' efficiency and to urge their transformation. The first was deregulation, granting the SOEs more autonomy, followed by invigorating the large enterprises while reducing control over the small ones. After that, a further measure was to introduce market competition while decreasing the monopoly of SOEs, through splitting the large SOEs into two or more smaller ones. With the concurrent legitimation of PEs, some small SOEs were transformed into PEs, while some others were merged into large SOEs.

Since the global financial crisis in the late 1990s, SOEs have become a major player in China's economy again. Large SOEs supported by policy banks emerged as the leaders in implementing China's "going out" policy through overseas direct investment with the purpose of acquiring foreign companies as well as seeking natural resources and markets. Meanwhile, in response to the indigenous innovation strategy, SOEs were expected to play a leading role in mega projects such as high-speed rail, nuclear power plants, and ultra-high voltage power transmission. During the global financial crisis in 2008, the central government, led by the Hu–Wen administration,[1] increased financial support to stimulate China's economy, most of which was allocated to giant SOEs for completing large-scale infrastructure projects. This, in turn, spurred further expansion of these SOEs.

Chinese SOEs have multiple objectives, not just profit maximization. This is the main reason why Chinese SOEs are usually regarded as inefficient and dawdling in adapting to a market regime. This assumption is based on SOEs requiring a large volume of input without yielding corresponding output (Hovey et al., 2003). Even so, up to this day, SOEs continue to play a key role in China's economy after more than three decades of experimental and gradual reform. The clear message is that the Chinese government will not eliminate SOEs; rather, it will preserve them as long as possible.

The Irreplaceable Role of SOEs

SOEs have strong implications for China's economy. They benefit from direct and indirect subsidies in terms of production factors (capital, energy, and land), regulatory preferences, and public procurement, which allow them to maintain their dominant positions in the pillar industries of the national economy. Despite the private sector's mass expansion during the later period of the Hu–Wen administration, SOEs continued to be a significant factor in China's economy in terms of output, profit, and employment. In addition, in the past decades, mergers among SOEs became prevalent, such as the merger of China Metallurgical Group and China Minmetals Corporation, Baosteel Group and Wuhan Iron and Steel Group, as well as China North Railway and China South Railway. Thus, the number of large SOEs under the State-Owned Assets Supervision and Administrative Commission (SASAC) fell from 196 in 2003 (when SASAC was established) to 96 in 2019.

---

[1]   The Hu–Wen administration represents the fourth generation of Chinese leadership. It is named after the surnames of two leaders, the Party General Secretary and President Hu Jintao, and government Premier Wen Jiabao.

The existing SOEs' overall productivity has continued to increase since the reform, and the gap of productivity between the SOEs and PEs, as well as foreign enterprises (FEs), has been narrowing. Figure 2.1 shows a sharp increase in SOEs' profitability in recent years; and it seems that SOEs' total profits may exceed those of PEs and FEs in the near future.

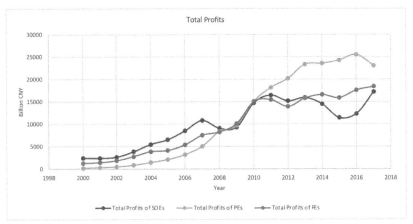

Source: National Bureau of Statistics of China (2014–2018).

Figure 2.1   *Total profits of different types of enterprises*

The revenue achievements of SOEs can be seen in the Fortune 500 list for 2019. Approximately 129 Chinese firms are listed, surpassing the United States (US) (121 firms) for the first time. Among the 129 Chinese firms, 48 are SOEs, and the top four Chinese SOEs in terms of annual revenue are SINOPEC Group (No. 2/500, US$414.65 billion), China National Petroleum (No. 4, US$392.98 billion), State Grid Corporation of China (No. 5, US$387.1 billion), and China State Construction Engineering (No. 21, US$181.5 billion). Moreover, many locally managed SOEs (supervised by SASAC at the provincial or municipal level), such as SAIC Group, are on that list as well.

2.2   BIRTH OF THE DUAL INNOVATION SYSTEMS

The main difference between the planned economy and the market economy is not whether or not it is a scientific or reasonable plan, but whether resources are allocated by administrative power or by market players' independent choice (Lewis, 2013).

From 1949 to 1978, SOEs held a dominant position; in fact, they were the only legitimate economic entities in China's economic system. The giant national projects and all resources were concentrated in state-owned enterprises, while PEs had not yet played a role in Chinese economic development. At this stage, although there was no specific concept of innovation or creation, authorities still achieved the goal of stimulating technological progress by increasing the number of technology imports and providing research funding (Chen and Chen, 2010). Some industries, such as coal mining, construction, large machinery and agriculture, were developing rapidly during this period. However, most industries lacked market vitality. Therefore, during this period, the overall development of the national innovation system lagged behind significantly (Liu and White, 2001).

In 1978, PEs started to play a role in China's innovation system. In the 1980s, the goal of the "institutional reform strategy" was to establish a modern enterprise system in SOEs, to push them to respond to market needs and to correct the agency problem by acknowledging the concept of property rights (Huang and Yu, 2013). Since then, private and non-public enterprises have been given a clear legal position as an important part of the Chinese economy. Meanwhile, many SOEs were allowed to be transformed into private enterprises. Some, however, were bankrupted because they were unable to attract the necessary talents and meet the needs of consumers in a competitive market (Shao, 2015). Figure 2.2 shows the growing number of registered PEs.

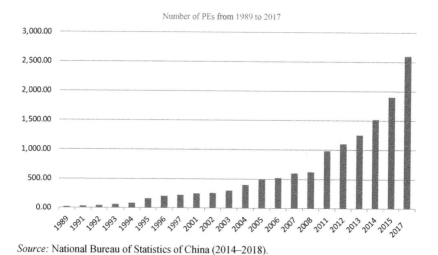

Source: National Bureau of Statistics of China (2014–2018).

Figure 2.2   Number of PEs from 1989 to 2017

From 1998 to 2000, SOEs experienced a big wave of major reform to deal with the nationwide inefficiency; that is, invigorating large SOEs while relaxing control over small ones (*zhua da fang xiao*). In line with this strategy, the number of state-owned enterprises decreased by 42 percent, and the number of laid-off workers reached more than 30 million. This situation gave birth to a large number of PEs. Nevertheless, the surviving SOEs became larger and larger, as many mergers and acquisitions followed; most of them in banking, utilities, telecommunications, construction, and the energy industry, that the government never tried to open to private enterprises. Two different but intertwined logics have been behind the reform of SOEs from the 1980s to the present: the political or state logic, that SOEs must take responsibility for national or political interests; and the market logic, to ensure that SOEs operate with the efficiency of private companies.

In 2003, SASAC, a milestone in the development of SOEs, was established, allowing the central government to strengthen its monitoring of state assets. Following this logic, in 2004, being restructured as modern enterprises became a new goal for SOEs to achieve. This required SOEs to have clear ownership and governance (to deal with the issue of principal–agency) as well as explicit power and responsibility. It also required the separation of governmental administration and enterprise management. After that, many large SOEs or centrally managed SOEs began to be listed on the capital markets. Currently, 70 percent of listed SOEs are centrally rather than regionally managed.

However, in 2012, a new strategy of SOE governance was established. The central government worried that there was too much corruption in SOEs, and many top management teams had salaries as high as those of the boards of directors for listed companies. Thus, the central government installed government officials as chief executive officers (CEOs) and directors on the boards of SOEs. In a sense, the governance of SOEs is now more in line with the state logic than with the market logic. Yet, at the same time, the government also tried to make SOEs more innovative. For example, in order to design better incentives for employees, on August 17, 2018, SASAC passed "The Guideline for SOEs' Employee Stock Ownership Plan," stating that the total employees' stock ownership cannot surpass 30 percent of total stock assets, and the chairman's portion cannot exceed 1 percent.

Meanwhile, since the late 1990s, PEs have entered a fast-growth stage. Many PEs emerged in industries such as real estate, steel, cement, chemicals, decorative materials, and light industry. According to the 2002 China Private Enterprise Survey Report, from 1991 to 2001 the annual growth rate in the number of PEs, registered capital, and household capital reached 34.08 percent, 64.81 percent, and 23.58 percent, respectively. The private sector's tax revenue grew at an average annual rate of 80.33 percent, making it the most dynamic and fastest-growing compared to other sectors.

In the meantime, the old laws and regulations that once hindered the development of PEs were largely abolished or revised; market access conditions were greatly relaxed; and the infrastructure industry was opened to PEs. In 2004, 2006, and 2009, respectively, the small and medium-sized enterprise (SME) board market, the new over-the-counter (OTC) market and the second-board market were established. These new capital markets further expanded the financing channels of PEs (Howie, 2011), and the systemic policies and events promoted the innovation and development in sectors of the private economy.

The different innovation models of SOEs and PEs can be traced back to their histories. The differences were obvious in the fundamental characteristics of the earliest stage of China's transition from central planning to greater market coordination and decentralized decision-making (Broadman, 1995; Steinfeld, 1998; White and Liu, 1998).

From 1949 to the 1980s, SOEs were operated without research and development (R&D) and sales divisions, or efficiency-based criteria for operational performance. SOEs were specialized "factories" whose activities and interactions would be managed by the central government; even the relevant R&D departments were controlled by different levels of governmental applied research institutes outside the SOEs (Liu and White, 2001).

In order to strengthen innovation capabilities at the firm level, in 1999, the central government inaugurated the transformation of governmental applied research institutes. These institutes were merged with large SOEs or directly transformed into independent SOEs. For example, the National Institute of Automobiles in Changchun was later merged with the First Automobile Group located in the same city. These reforms also resulted in the establishment of R&D divisions within the organizational structures of large SOEs, such as the Shanghai Baosteel Group. Most of the 260 transformed central research institutes have survived. Some have become leading technology-based companies, such as GRINM Group and Shanghai Electric Group. Most of the transformed research institutes still maintain close connections with those manufacturing SOEs as their product users, such as Datang with China Telecom, China Mobile, and China Unicom (Du, 2009).

Comparatively, PEs in China do not have a long history of R&D activities. Yet they have more capabilities to take advantage of the windows of opportunity in terms of both market and technology. They also learn from the practices of foreign companies how to build their own innovation systems. Huawei is a good example: the company's innovation system owes a lot – such as the deployment of its famous integrated product development (IPD) – to IBM's consultancy.

Innovations of PEs and SOEs are different in their nature and sector focus. Some PEs tend to focus on the lighting and household appliance sector, while some are good at taking advantage of new technologies with the information revolution and Internet economy. A number of private IT enterprises, such as Netease, Sohu, Sina, Baidu, and Alibaba, were born due to the new windows of technological opportunity. After nearly 20 years of development, these companies have grown to lead the Chinese and even the global Internet economy. They have nurtured a number of world-class unicorns controlled by Alibaba. Moreover, leading Chinese PEs also have integrated into the globalization process and participated in more international competition than SOEs. SOEs' and PEs' innovation inputs (in terms of R&D expenditures) and outputs (patents) can be seen in Figure 2.3 and Figure 2.4.

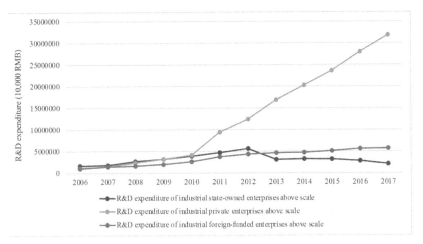

Figure 2.3   *The R&D expenditures of SOEs, private enterprises, and foreign enterprises*

2.3   DIFFERENT FEATURES OF THE TWO ENTITIES IN THE DUAL INNOVATION SYSTEMS

We have shown that both SOEs and PEs have played an irreplaceable role in the Chinese dual innovation systems, learning from each other and developing together (Liu, 2006). The major differences regarding their innovations are a further topic, addressed in this section.

Different Levels of Innovation Openness

Mostly, innovation in SOEs is somewhat more closed, while innovation of PEs is more open. PEs are new to the industry and have to be more open so as to mobilize the necessary resources. Thus, they make great efforts to tap global resources and innovations from various enterprises and scientific research

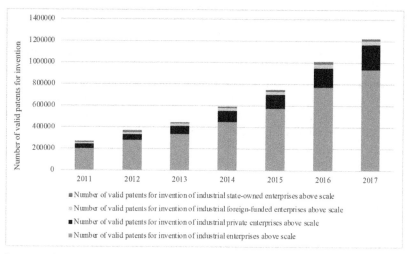

Source: National Bureau of Statistics of China (2014–2018).

Figure 2.4   *Patents of SOEs, private enterprises, and foreign enterprises in China*

institutions and to gain knowledge from experts and scholars (Chesbrough et al., 2006). By tapping the domestic market and deploying the "amphibious strategy" in international markets, PEs try to enhance their global influence. For example, over 70 percent of Huawei's market share actually is overseas, and more breakthrough innovations in 5G were accomplished by established world-class R&D laboratories.

SOEs are usually slow to go global, though they have more early experience in doing so than PEs. Table 2.1 shows some of the first overseas investment projects of SOEs from 1995 to 2000. For example, in the 1990s, some home appliance manufacturers began direct investment in Southeast Asia (Liu, 2018). However, these experiences have not allowed SOEs to fully participate in the international competition. The share of foreign direct investment stock of SOEs fell from 81 percent in 2006 to 50.4 percent in 2015. In 2016, the foreign direct investment of SOEs was US$57.99 billion, while the foreign direct investment of PEs reached US$123.24 billion.

Different Driving Forces of Innovation

SOEs' innovation is largely led and incentivized by the government, while PEs' innovation is usually driven by dynamic market changes. Most SOEs

Table 2.1   *The first overseas investment projects of SOEs from 1995 to 2000*

SOEs	Year	Host country	Content
Little Swan Company	1995	Malaysia	Building a home appliance factory
Hisense Group	1996	South Africa	Building a home appliance factory
Jincheng Corporation	1996	Colombia	Establishing a motorcycle factory
TCL Group	1996	Vietnam	Acquisition of DONACO (a color TV production enterprise)
CWGC (China Worldbest Group)	1997	Niger	Acquisition of a textile factory
Konka Group	1998	Indonesia	Building a home appliance factory
Chunlan Group	1999	Spain, Iran	Establishing a motorcycle factory
Gree Group	1999	Brazil	Building an electric appliance factory
Changhong Group	2000	Indonesia	Building a home appliance assembly factory

have a special mission: to maintain and increase the value of national assets. The CEOs and senior managers of state-owned enterprises are selected and assigned by the government. If the business is operated well, they will get promotions in a political sense instead of a direct financial reward. Due to heavy administrative limitations, SOE managers are not promoted due to their performance of business operations, but rather, due to their administrative qualifications and the SOEs' implementation of political missions. Thus, SOEs tend to adhere to state logic, while PEs are developed with more market logic.

Innovation in PEs comes from market competition and entrepreneurship (Schumpeter, 1912). Haier's "micro enterprises" (MEs) and "entrepreneurship at scale" are typical examples of market-driven principles. Haier breaks the traditional bureaucracy and forms an open entrepreneurial ecosystem platform, creating countless self-employed, self-organizing, and self-driven small and micro enterprises. This system enables everyone in the ecosystem to face the market and users and create value with independence (Hamel and Zanini, 2018). MEs determine resources and business arrangements according to their goals of satisfying customers' needs. The salary distribution is leveraged by the employees' value in meeting users' needs. The drive to satisfy all customers inspires more outstanding employees to invest in the future of the innovation ecosystem, which makes it possible for Haier's model to remain competitive in the long run (Pinchot and Pinchot, 1994).

Different Sources of Innovation Resources

State-owned enterprises' innovation is usually based on a combination of internal existing resources and external monopolized resources that can be obtained under government protection; while PEs rely more on their own resources for innovation (David et al., 2000). Indeed, SOEs enjoy the inherent advantages of financing (Figure 2.5). For example, despite their high-level debt, SOEs can obtain bank loans at a much lower interest rate than PEs and others, while PEs usually cannot enjoy such preferential policies.

Nonetheless, the missions that SOEs carry out have become increasingly complicated and ambitious, especially indigenous innovation. On the one hand, compared to the PEs and FEs, SOEs lack incentives to increase productivity and profitability, as well as to meet all the sophisticated criteria of innovation. On the other hand, to execute the mission of indigenous innovation imposed by the state, SOEs usually have to mobilize financial resources and take risks to support innovation in national projects (often at a loss), which in turn may help to generate large financial returns in other projects (Naughton, 2018). It seems that this dilemma will not allow the indigenous innovation in SOEs to be sustainable; not to mention other challenging targets such as gaining global competitiveness and leading global mega-projects.

In terms of talent resources, it is undeniable that PEs were weak at first. To improve this situation, many of them hired talented people or used brain-drain strategy to learn the latest technologies. Many successful Chinese PEs' entrepreneurs are former technology experts or engineers of SOEs or governmental research institutes. A good example is the founder of Huawei, Ren Zhengfei, who used to be an engineer of an SOE. Another example is the founder of Lenovo, Liu Chuanzhi, who was a researcher of an institute of the Chinese Academy of Sciences.

2.4   INTERACTIONS IN THE DUAL INNOVATION SYSTEMS

The dual innovation systems work in a parallel way with certain interactions in various industries. The relationship between the types of activities that organizations undertake may differ in terms of the industries involved.

In SOE-Monopolizing Industries

In the infrastructure and utilities industries strongly related to the national interest, SOEs have monopolistic control (Shi and Zhong, 2018). The industries have three typical characteristics. First, the scale of investment is huge, the payback period is long, and the profitability is low. Second, they provide

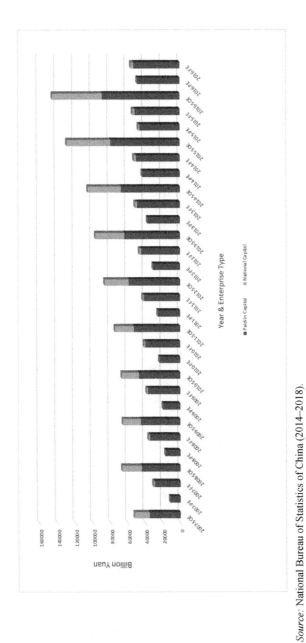

Source: National Bureau of Statistics of China (2014–2018).

Figure 2.5   *Paid-in capital and national capital of different types of enterprises*

public goods, so the social benefits are far greater than the private economic benefits. Third, they have monopolistic features, and if PEs are allowed to operate in those industries, in order to gain high profits the PEs may take actions undermining the required social benefits (Cao et al., 2011). Therefore, these industries are dominated by SOEs. However, they cannot be completely monopolized by SOEs. Thus, many PEs became the suppliers for SOEs, and the two types of enterprises work together to create value for customers.

In Competitive Industries

In some industries, such as automobiles, chemicals, and steel, SOEs and PEs may compete intensively with each other. These industries were originally dominated by SOEs, but the reform of China's economic system allowed PEs to enter, thus triggering competition. For example, in the steel industry the majority of firms are SOEs, but one private enterprise, the Shagang Group, is also quite competitive. In the automobile industry, which SOEs used to dominate, private manufacturers such as Geely and BYD have become competitive players in recent years.

In Emerging Industries

Industries that are highly uncertain require entrepreneurship and demand firms' fast responses to market needs. Under these circumstances, PEs are more likely to lead. Lenovo is a representative PE in the personal computer (PC) industry. Following decades of development, Lenovo became the PC world leader. In the telecommunications industry, the operators are all SOEs, but PEs such as Huawei have gained a strong foothold in hardware manufacture, including system equipment, switchers, and handsets. In the arena of e-commerce, SOEs have almost no position, while Ali and Tencent are powerful players.

Similarly, in industries that meet consumers' daily needs, such as home appliances, food, garments, and furniture, SOEs originally had some leadership. Over time, however, they retreated, and PEs became the major players, such as Haier and Midea which have become global leaders.

REFERENCES

Brilhuis-Meijer, E., Pigosso, D.C., and McAloone, T.C. (2016). Integrating product and technology development: A proposed reference model for dual innovation. *Procedia Cirp, 50,* 32–37.
Broadman, H.G. (1995). *Meeting the Challenge of Chinese Enterprise Reform.* Washington, DC: World Bank.

Cao, J., Pan, X., and Tian, G. (2011). Disproportional ownership structure and pay–performance relationship: Evidence from China's listed firms. *Journal of Corporate Finance*, *17*(3), 541–554.

Chen, L., and Chen, Y. (2010). *Concerto for Mutual Benefit: State-Owned Enterprise's Innovation Ability and Innovation Support*. Beijing: Economic Management Press.

Chesbrough, H., Vanhaverbeke, W., and West, J. (eds) (2006). *Open Innovation: Researching a New Paradigm*. Oxford University Press on Demand.

David, P.A., Hall, B.H., and Toole, A.A. (2000). Is public R&D a complement or substitute for private R&D? A review of the econometric evidence. *Research Policy*, *29*(4–5), 497–529.

Du, Y. (2009). Datong is different – interpretation of China's three major telecom operators' 2009 work conference. *China Telecom Industry*, *2*, 32–33.

Hamel, G., and Zanini, M. (2018). The end of bureaucracy. *Harvard Business Review*, *96*(6), 50–59.

Hovey, M., Li, L., and Naughton, T. (2003). The relationship between valuation and ownership of listed firms in China. *Corporate Governance: An International Review*, *11*(2), 112–122.

Howie, F.J. (2011). *Privatizing China: Inside China's Stock Markets*. Singapore: John Wiley & Sons.

Huang, Q. and Yu, J. (2013). New ideas in the new era: Classification reform and governance of state-owned enterprises. *China Industrial Economy*, *11*, 5–17.

Lewis, W.A. (2013). *Principles of Economic Planning*. London, UK and New York, USA: Routledge.

Liu, J. (2018). 40 years of internationalization of state-owned enterprises: Development history and its institutional logic. *Economics and Management Research*, *10*, 13–30.

Liu, X. (2006). The dualistic Chinese innovation system (in Chinese). *Science of Science and Technology Management*, *2*, 14–22.

Liu, X., and White, S. (2001). Comparing innovation systems: A framework and application to China's transitional context. *Research Policy*, *30*(7), 1091–1114.

Majocchi, A., and Strange, R. (2012). International diversification. *Management International Review*, *52*(6), 879–900.

Megginson, W.L., and Netter, J.M. (2001). From state to market: A survey of empirical studies on privatization. *Journal of Economic Literature*, *39*(2), 321–389.

National Bureau of Statistics of China (2014–2018). *The China Statistical Yearbook 2013–2017*. Beijing: China Statistics Press.

Naughton, B. (2018). Presentation in Forum in Memorandum of China Opening of Forty Years. Beijing, December 22.

Pinchot, G., and Pinchot, E. (1994). *The End of Bureaucracy and the Rise of the Intelligent Organization*. San Francisco, CA: Berrett-Koehler Publishers.

Schumpeter, J.A. (1912). *Theorie der Wirtschaftlichen Entwicklung* (in German). Leipzig: Dunker & Humblot.

Shao, N. (2015). Analysis of the situation of state-owned enterprise reform. Speech at the 98th "Development Salon" organized by the Shanghai Development Foundation.

Shi, W., and Zhong, C. (2018). *Blue Book of State-Owned Enterprises*. Beijing: Social Sciences Academic Press.

Steinfeld, E.S. (1998). *Forging Reform in China: The Fate of State-Owned Industry*. Cambridge: Cambridge University Press.

White, S., and Liu, X. (1998). Organizational processes to meet new performance criteria: Chinese pharmaceutical firms in transition. *Research Policy*, *27*(4), 369–383.

3. State Grid and user-driven innovation: the case of ultra-high voltage power transmission

The innovation ecosystem is a network of interconnected organizations consisting of producers, users, and complementors. Coordinated by a focal firm or a platform, the network exchanges, creates, and appropriates value through innovation (Autio and Thomas, 2014; Teece, 2007; Cusumano and Gawer, 2002; Gawer and Cusumano, 2002). Facing the current fierce competition, enterprises are becoming interdependent components of this innovation ecosystem: different from the conventional geographically clustered producers, which are usually homogeneous. On the one hand, they improve technological competencies through innovation at the ecosystem level (Moore, 1993); on the other hand, they unite to deal with competition outside the current ecosystem (Iansiti and Levien, 2004). Within the innovation ecosystem, enterprises jointly innovate and create value by exchanging complementary values, capabilities, and resources (Adner and Kapoor, 2010). Besides value co-creation based on common interests, the ecosystem actors also consider their own value capture within the ecosystem. As interests and goals between ecosystem actors are always partially aligned, the co-existence of cooperative behaviors to create value and competitive behaviors to capture value leads to a compromise between cooperation and competition, and merges into something called "coopetition" (Bengtsson and Kock, 2000; Brandenburger and Nalebuff, 1996). This concept challenges the classic theory of competitive advantage, which highlights competition between industrial players and emphasizes lowering the bargaining power of a focal firm's suppliers, customers, and complementors through acquiring an advantageous industrial position (Hearn and Pace, 2006).

While innovation ecosystems are evolving, the traditional technology-oriented and manufacturer-centered innovation modes are altered, and users play an increasingly important role. In some ecosystems, users may even play the key role as an orchestrator that guides and coordinates the relevant actors in the system. In this chapter, we will scrutinize how a technological leader and key user, State Grid, successfully bridged and united the divergent innovation actors to jointly realize a common value proposition, that is, ultra-high voltage power transmission (UHV).

The data for this chapter mainly came from a day of interviews, on July 7, 2015, with State Grid's high-level managers at the company's headquarters in Beijing, as well as from its internal reports and some of its published reports.

3.1 USERS' ROLE IN THE INNOVATION ECOSYSTEM

A number of studies have investigated different possible configurations of the innovation ecosystem, underlining the contributions of complementary firms and auxiliary assets to the ecosystems' development (Adner and Kapoor, 2010; Kapoor and Lee, 2013). However, with the rapid development of information technologies (IT), other stakeholders, such as users, financial enterprises, research institutes, universities, and the government, have begun to play indispensable roles in the ecosystems' formation and development. It is now common to see users participating in product conception, design, manufacture and improvement, and this trend is, in turn, facilitating the flattening and opening of the producers' organizational structure. New business models, such as crowdfunding, crowdsourcing, and crowd-creating, are changing the closed resource allocation model in industries, as well as enabling intellectual resources and social capital to freely flow for new innovation ecosystems' development.

Although upstream partners of a core enterprise in an ecosystem may bring in key resources and add value through innovations of technology and component, downstream customers may also add value via applications, demand, and infrastructure for the industrial chain's maturation. Compared to the more traditional notion of a producer-driven value-adding process, a user-driven innovation ecosystem may help the enterprises be better aligned with market trends and be more agile in their integration of the resources required for innovation. The concept and trend of user innovation stem from von Hippel's (1976) viewpoint that "users are innovators," where users are regarded as the essential source of innovation (Lettl et al., 2006). User innovation is also seen as a symbol of the democratization of innovation (von Hippel, 2005), compared to the producer-centered or producer-driven innovation (von Hippel, 1986).

State Grid Corporation of China, derived from a governmental institute – the (former) Electric Power Department of the (former) Ministry of Water Resources and Electricity – was founded on December 29, 2002 to lead and carry out large-scale infrastructure projects to reconstruct the national electric power system. Currently, it is a large state-owned enterprise (SOE) that functions as an electric power transmitter, with 1.63 million employees and 829.5 billion RMB of registered capital, and it exercises part of the government administrative functions. Further, State Grid is also the world's largest utility company and the world's second-largest company by annual revenue.

State Grid's core businesses are construction and operation of the national power grid for 1.1 billion people in 26 provinces, autonomous regions and municipalities, covering 88 percent of the Chinese national territory.[1] As a Chinese SOE, State Grid also owns and operates overseas branches and assets in countries such as the Philippines, Brazil, Portugal, Australia, and Italy. In its 16 years of development, State Grid has successfully accomplished a historically groundbreaking innovation in electric power transmission: the ultra-high voltage (UHV) power transmission. This project is a good example of large SOEs' user-driven collaborative innovation. Specifically, the UHV power transmission project is a typical complex product system (CoPS): it has a long industrial chain with large numbers of interdependent actors, high-level technological complexity, rigorous safety requirements, and high demand for suppliers' technical capacities. The complex nature of a CoPS project, along with all of the required high standards, determines the necessity and importance of collaborative innovation throughout the whole industrial chain, based on the end-user's demand and core player's leadership. In this infrastructure innovation project, State Grid played as end-user, facilitating, catalyzing, and supervising the progress with its large pool of capital and resources.

3.2   STATE GRID'S UHV TRANSMISSION PROJECT

At the end of 2004, State Grid proposed the development of the UHV transmission strategy based on the nation's increasing electric power demand, along with China's economic boom and the long distance between energy providers and consumers. The strategy proposed a national-level, reliable smart grid with a UHV electrified wire network as its backbone and a harmoniously developed smart grid at all levels as its strong foundation. With such a grid in place, the construction of and synergy among mega-hydropower, coal-fired power, nuclear power, and renewable energy power bases could be achieved. These strategic actions and infrastructure projects could support the central government's national strategy, help to optimize energy and resource allocation across the country, as well as achieve large-scale and long-distance transmission, and ensure the sustainable power needed for economic and social development.

With systematic coordination and collaboration, the UHV project has accomplished comprehensive breakthroughs in the areas of power grid technology, electrical equipment, and project construction and operation. State

---

[1]   http://en.chinapower.com.cn/2015/05/28/content_2725.html.

Grid thus attained a worldwide leading position in the key technologies of UHV transmission, equipment development, and engineering applications. Furthermore, as an important part of the Chinese national energy development strategy on better allocation of nationwide energy resources, the UHV project is also a good example of national strategic innovation.

UHV alternating current (AC) transmission refers to the transmission on the voltage level of 1000 kV and above. Compared with the ordinary 500 kV AC transmission, the UHV transmission power is four to five times higher, and the transmission distance is two to three times longer. Yet the transmission loss is only one-third to one-quarter, and the transmission corridor width is only half to one-third. In short, the technology has the prominent advantages of large capacity, long distance, low loss, and a small footprint (hence, land saving). However, the ultra-high voltage transmission is not merely a simple amplification of high voltage transmission; rather, it is based on systematic research that aims to address four major technical issues:

- Voltage control. As mentioned, the UHV system has a large capacity and covers long distances. Under normal circumstances, the maximum voltage is controlled below 1100 kV, and the voltage distribution is balanced. However, when disconnection happens, the voltage distribution changes suddenly, and the terminal voltage uplifts sharply, directly threatening the system's stability and the equipment's safety.
- Difficulty in configuring external insulation. The UHV system's external insulation is large, and the line tower is high, greatly increasing the probability of lightning strikes. Moreover, China has serious atmospheric pollution, causing insulators to be prone to surface flashover: an electric discharge over or around the surface of an insulator.
- Difficulty in controlling the electromagnetic environment. The multi-conductor system composed of large-sized UHV transmission lines and substations likely causes conductor interactions. Thus, the electric field intensity of the charged conductor's surface and surrounding space increases significantly, and the audible noise and radio interference caused by the electric discharge – known as the corona discharge – are prominent.
- Difficulty in equipment development. UHV equipment includes 40 types in nine categories. It is challenging to balance the intensities of the electric, magnetic, and thermal fields. Simple amplification based on existing technology will lead to oversized equipment, and thus to high production costs and low transportability.

The development of the UHV transmission technology required the work of more than 100 business branches and units of State Grid, nearly 50 000 people from the company's research and development (R&D), design, and manufacture units, as well as external partners such as universities. The project involved 180 key research subjects and the development of 40 kinds of equipment in nine categories. State Grid and its partners achieved six major technological breakthroughs and 96 patents, including those for voltage control, external insulation configuration, electromagnetic environment control, complete equipment development, system integration, and test capacity.

In 2014, the key technologies, complete equipment and engineering applications of UHV AC transmission won the special prize of the National Science and Technology Progress Award, the highest science and technology honor awarded to State Grid so far. Since 2009, without the adverse impact of the international financial crisis, exports of the UHV equipment have been increasing: total exports have been over 10 billion yuan, and the annual growth rate has been over 40 percent. Furthermore, State Grid has developed a comprehensive model of "user-driven innovation management." With this model, it took State Grid less than four years to address the major technical challenges. In addition, the company has made a range of world-class records in ±800 kV UHV DC transmission, UHV AC series compensation, UHV AC double-circuit transmission, high-end power transmission and transformation equipment manufacturing, and other pertinent high-tech fields.

3.3 THE SHARED GOAL ACROSS THE INNOVATION ECOSYSTEM

With China's fast development in the first decade of the 21st century, the market demand shifted from primary consumer goods to advanced consumer goods, implying that the quality and technical attributes of products and services would greatly increase in the Chinese market. With the upgrading demands, requiring more electric power was inevitable, especially in the areas with a higher volume of power consumption: areas that were usually economically fast-growing or well-developed. However, the area with most (electric) power consumption is geographically distant from the one with highest power generation (for example, hydropower, wind power, and solar power) in China: that is, the former is along the east coast, while the latter is located in China's "Wild West." How to transmit the abundant power produced in West China to meet the considerable power demands in East China became a major concern for the government, and addressing the national strategic concern became the shared goal across the innovation ecosystem.

As the implementer of the government's comprehensive plans for economic and social sustainable development, State Grid addressed the above-mentioned societal and governmental concerns by developing a preliminary scheme of the UHV project, and it proactively sought government support for the project. At the end of 2004, State Grid comprehensively demonstrated the need to develop

UHV power transmission technology that would address the national issue of power insufficiency in East China. The company reported this to the government and promoted relevant authentication. After the authentication was completed, the UHV project was included in a series of major national strategic plans for development, such as the National Medium- and Long-Term Plan for Science and Technology Development, the Opinions of the State Council on Accelerating the Revitalization of the Equipment Manufacturing Industry, the National Eleventh Five-Year Plan for Building Fundamental Capacity of Independent Innovation, and China's National Climate Change Program. The project received most of its financial support from the National Development and Reform Commission and the Ministry of Science and Technology.

In August 2006, the 1000 kV Jindongnan–Jinmen UHV AC pilot demonstration project was approved as a support project for China's development of UHV transmission technology, and on January 6, 2009, it was completed and put into operation. The project has passed a range of inspections on water and environment protection, scientific and technological breakthrough, localization of equipment manufacture, and project archives, organized by the Ministry of Water Resources, the Ministry of Environmental Protection, the Ministry of Science and Technology, the State Archives Administration, and the National Development and Reform Commission. In 2010, expansion of the UHV AC pilot demonstration project was approved (for example, from Huainan to Shanghai, and from northern Zhejiang to Fuzhou). This expansion has created a widespread consensus on UHV's role in energy security, smog control, energy efficiency improvement, and economic and social development. Furthermore, eight UHV projects have been added into the 2018 National Air Pollution Prevention Action Plan, indicating the large-scale implementation of UHV technology in China.

Based on the ever-increasing demand for electric energy that comes with economic growth, the world's electric power development focuses on improving the reliability and efficiency of the power supply. Technical challenges arise when attempting to improve transmission capacity, expand geographic range of power transmission, and reduce costs and energy loss during the transmission.

The history of the power grid shows that when the power load increases by 5–10 percent, the grid voltage will increase to a new level in 15–25 years. Moreover, more than 70 percent of China's electricity demand is concentrated in Central and East China, but the power resources are abundant in the Northwest, North, and Southwest. Seventy-six percent of the coal reserves are concentrated in North and Northwest China, while 80 percent of hydropower resources are in the Southwest. Different types of energy resources are rather scattered. For a long time, China's energy and electric power supply has been self-sufficient only at the local level, instead of coordinated and balanced at the national level.

For example, a large number of thermal power plants are located in the eastern and central regions (the current installed capacity of East China, North China, and Central China are all over 200 million kW), and the energy allocation is excessively dependent on coal transportation, in spite of the rather unbalanced energy conversion ratio of coal to electricity, which is 20:1. As a result, the tension between coal transportation and electricity transmission – along with environmental pressures – is increasing in East China. To protect the environment, the government is not allowing more coal-fired power plants to be built. Similarly, most land-based wind and solar power and hydropower generators concentrate in the North and West, and thus electric power needs to be transmitted over long distances. The newly planned nuclear power plants will be located mainly in Central China, also requiring strong grid support for transmission. In short, China's energy production center and consumption areas can be 800–3000 kilometers apart, and large-scale and long-distance power transmission is therefore necessary.

From another perspective, although the voltage level of the existing main grid in China is 500 kV, after more than 30 years of development, the total installed power grid capacity is 15.3 times larger than before. The number of State Grid's 500 kV substations has reached 353, and the transmission distance has exceeded 100 000 kilometers, but the average distance between the substations is 90 kilometers, and in the Yangtze River Delta region the average distance is smaller. Due to the concerns such as short-circuit current, shortage of land resources, and environmental protection, it is also reasonable to develop new technology that supports large-capacity, long-distance, and high-efficiency power transmission, so as to achieve better power allocation across a wider area of China. Compared with the highest voltage level in foreign power grids, which is 750 kV, UHV AC transmission is a technology with an even higher voltage level. It represents the most advanced high voltage transmission technology and addresses a range of the most challenging technical issues, such as high-level voltage and current, severe natural environments, electromagnetic interference, and insulation. Even though the (former) Soviet Union, Japan, Italy, and the United States conducted preliminary UHV research between the 1960s and 1990s, they failed due to limitations of technology and equipment. The development of UHV transmission technology is largely a systematic engineering process, following the technological trends and demand evolution.

3.4 COORDINATION IN THE ECOSYSTEM AND COLLABORATIVE INNOVATION

With the central government's support, State Grid initiated the innovation consortium of the UHV Transmission Project (Figure 3.1) which gathered key resources in research, design, equipment manufacture, and engineering and construction, aiming to eliminate the upstream–downstream barriers so as to strengthen knowledge sharing and collaboration on the key technologies. This innovation consortium surrounding the key value proposition of UHV Transmission is also in line with the innovation ecosystem that we describe in this book.

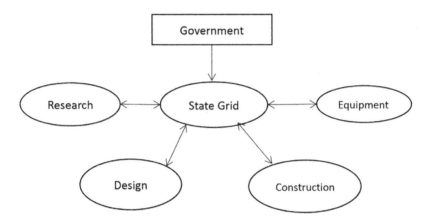

Figure 3.1   The innovation consortium of the UHV AC Power Transmission Project

Essentially, State Grid was the initiator of the innovation value chain, as well as the organizer, participant, guarantor, and decision-maker of the innovation process and the institutional user of the developed technology. Its member companies were the first users of the mutual innovation outputs and advocates of the large-scale commercial applications. State Grid analyzed and determined overall objectives of the innovation consortium: to fully master the key technologies of UHV AC transmission system; and to realize independent innovation through research and planning, system and engineering design, equipment manufacturing, and construction and maintenance, so as to complete a high-quality project that is safe, reliable, innovative, economical, environmentally friendly and global-leading. Through the consortium, State Grid developed an effective ecosystem of organizations with unified command and intensive control (Figure 3.2 and Table 3.1). It effectively integrated the strength of more than 100 organizations in the electric power and machinery industries of China and provided a solid institutional foundation for collaborative innovation. Moreover, State Grid developed a particular mechanism for efficiently organizing, cooperatively operating, and jointly making decisions, which facilitated achieving the innovation ecosystem's predetermined target.

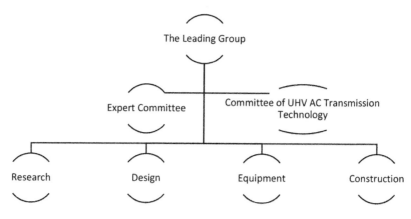

Figure 3.2   *The organizational structure of the ecosystem*

In 2004, when the UHV Power Transmission Project was first proposed, State Grid had established a leadership group for the project, under the leadership of General Manager Liu Zhenya. After approval by the government, State Grid's leadership group organized a test and demonstration project of the UHV. The major technical issues were assigned to experts and specialists, and the corresponding plans and schemes were submitted to the leadership group, which was responsible for reviewing the major technical plans and research results, making decisions, and coordinating and guiding the construction.

There were two subgroups of experts under the leadership group. One consisted of an expert committee as well as assembling academics and experts in the field of UHV transmission, who were responsible for examining and evaluating the major technical schemes. The other subgroup was the UHV AC Transmission Technology Standardization Committee, which was responsible for formulating relevant standards to guide the follow-up projects.

The State Grid headquarters established the UHV Construction Department, taking charge of the whole process management and supervision of the project

Table 3.1   Key functions and partners through the innovation process

Function	Partners	Function	Partners
Research	China Electric Power Research Institute	Equipment	XD Group
	State Grid Electric Power Research Institute		Baoding Tianwei Group
	State Grid Economic and Technological Research Institute		TBEA, Shenyang
	Xi'an High Voltage Apparatus Research Institute		TBEA, Hengyang
	Tsinghua University		Pinggao Group
	Xi'an Jiaotong University		Xi'an XD Switchgear Electric
	North China Electric Power University		NHVS
	Shanghai Jiaotong University		Fushun Electric Porcelain Manufacturing
	Huazhong University of Science and Technology		PG Toshiba (Langfang) Arrester
	Wuhan University		Xi'an XD High Voltage Porcelain Insulator
	Chongqing University		Guilin Power Capacitor
	Tongji University		Trench China MWB (Shanghai)
	Zhengzhou Research Institute of Mechanical Engineering		Changgao Electric Group
	Shenyang Transformer Research Institute		NARI Technology
			Beijing Sifang Automation
			NR Electric
			...

Catch-up and radical innovation in Chinese state-owned enterprises

Function	Partners
Design	China Power Engineering Consulting Group
	North China Electric Power Design Institute
	East China Electric Power Design Institute
	Central China Electric Power Design Institute
	Southwest Electric Power Design Institute
	Northwest Electric Power Design Institute
	Northeast Electric Power Design Institute
	Shanxi Electric Power Design Institute
	Henan Electric Power Design Institute
	Shandong Electric Power Design Institute
	Zhejiang Electric Power Design Institute
	Hubei Electric Power Design Institute
	Hunan Electric Power Design Institute
	Jiangsu Electric Power Design Institute
Construction	State Grid AC Power Construction Branch
	State Grid Shanxi Electric Power Company
	State Grid Hunan Electric Power
	State Grid Hubei Electric Power
	State Grid Information& Telecommunication Group
	Hunan Transmission and Transformation Construction Company
	Henan Transmission and Transformation Construction Company
	Anhui Transmission and Transformation Construction Company
	Hubei Transmission and Transformation Construction Company
	Shandong Transmission and Transformation Construction Company
	Shanxi Transmission and Transformation Construction Company
	Shanghai Transmission and Transformation Construction Company
	SDCX
	Zhejiang Zhongchao Construction Group
	Hunan Hydro & Power Project Consultation Company

construction. State Grid also established UHV units in its provincial-level companies, set up command centers at the construction sites, and thus developed a three-level system for the project construction that optimized its members' resources and capacities. Special groups were formed to develop specific solutions for all kinds of research, design, and equipment issues. In addition, other member organizations not belonging to State Grid also set up specialized teams for the collaborative innovation. Based on rigorous organization and careful planning, an efficient and orderly decision-making mechanism was formed.

First, the leading research institutes – at different levels and geographically dispersed – were connected with an open innovation model. The electric power research institutes (for example, China Electric Power Research Institute, Wuhan High Voltage Research Institute, Electric Power Construction Institute, and Nanjing Automation Research Institute), the machinery research institutes (for example, Xi'an High Voltage Apparatus Research Institute, Shenyang Transformer Research Institute, Zhengzhou Research Institute of Mechanical Engineering), and universities such as Tsinghua University and Xi'an Jiaotong University, collaborated to create a solid theoretical foundation for coping with the world-class challenges of UHV transmission.

Second, a joint design system was deployed. The established design consortium, led by State Grid, consisted of China Power Engineering Consulting Group, the six electric power design institutes in North, East, South, Northeast, Northwest, and Southwest China, and relevant partners in research, equipment manufacture, construction, and operations. Given the fact that there were no internationally available technological standards and engineering experience in UHV design, systematic integration for overall performance – including safety, reliability, economy, and operational flexibility – became pivotal. Specifically, a design group was established, including the key technical personnel from China Power Engineering Consulting Group and State Grid's six electric power design institutes. The design group was responsible, initially, for proposing key design principles and major plans; and later, for implementing the reviewed and examined principles and plans in their ongoing work. Thus, the traditional independent design mode was abandoned, and instead the UHV project synthesized high-quality design resources and wisdom to the greatest extent, and remarkably improved design efficiency.

Third, for joint development, State Grid united the major manufacturers of power transmission and transformation equipment, such as XD Group, TBEA, Baoding Tianwei Group, Pinggao Group, and NHVS; specialists and experts from universities and research institutes; and companies and units specializing in design, test, construction, and operations. This diverse group came together to exercise open and joint innovation based on experiences and lessons learned from developing similar equipment domestically and abroad.

Fourth, standardized project construction was promoted, and the management model combining specialization and localization was adopted. The construction division of State Grid organized on-site construction, while the provincial branch companies handled local affairs such as land acquisition and compensation. This deployed all parties' advantages and strengths, and created a joint force to solve any construction problems.

Instead of the common technology-push innovation starting with pure basic research, followed by gradually transforming the research discovery into technology, the UHV project was directly targeted to the specific market demand and its overall strategic objective. This targeted approach largely smoothed the subsequent engineering and construction, and even the rapid iteration. To a great extent, this facilitated close connections between all the aspects and elements at different stages, and optimized resource input, addressing the issues of financial shortage, innovation isolation, and scientific achievement transformation. Hence, the whole project was well supported by a series of experimental demonstration projects, which we describe below:

Developing Technical Standards to Guide Collaborative Innovation

First, approved by the National Standardization Committee, in February 2007, State Grid set up the UHV AC Transmission Standardization Technical Committee, comprising the China Electricity Council, China Machinery Industry Federation, and relevant experts and specialists. Combining the achievements of scientific research and engineering practice, the committee developed the UHV AC Transmission Technical Standard System consisting of 77 standards in electric power and energy industries, covering system integration, engineering design, equipment manufacturing, construction and installation, testing and debugging, and operation and maintenance. In December 2009, the National Standardization Committee awarded the UHV AC Transmission Technology the title of "National Demonstration of Major Project Standardization." This UHV transmission technical standard has been completely deployed in the lines from Huainan to Shanghai, and from North Zhejiang to Fuzhou. The International Conference on Large High Voltage Electric Systems and the Institute of Electrical and Electronic Engineers also established eight UHV units led by Chinese specialists to internationalize State Grid's technical standards of UHV AC Transmission. To a great extent, to effectively and efficiently achieve technical coordination for collaborative innovation in a meta-project like UHV Transmission, developing systematic technical standards is highly necessary.

Combining Technical Frameworks and Targeted Applications Based On Specific Technical Demands

In 2005, before the approval of the proposed UHV project, State Grid had started to assemble specialists and experts to comprehensively investigate the technical requirements of UHV transmission, and had proposed some relevant research frameworks and subjects. Accordingly, the UHV research project consisted of two parts: the first one was for UHV key technology research framework and subjects, supported by State Grid research funding; the second one required in-depth research based on specific demands of the engineering practices, including 71 separate research projects. The UHV research framework thus presented research targets for the project as a whole, as well as follow-up subprojects for solving specific problems in design, construction, operation, development, and organization.

Research

Based on in-depth research, State Grid developed the technological framework of UHV AC transmission, composed of 180 research subjects. It also organized all the research units and institutes for further research on the project's entire process, including planning, system development, technical design, equipment manufacture, engineering and construction, debugging, testing, and scheduling and operation (Figure 3.3). Sixteen of the subjects were included in the Major Projects of the National Science and Technology Support Program in the Eleventh Five-Year Plan. In addition to targeted basic research – such as large-sized equipment and joint effects of nonlinear electric, magnetic, thermal, and force fields – specialized research in engineering applications was especially strengthened. The special research subjects used to directly promote the application of basic research results accounted for 40 percent of the total subjects.

Design

First, the main design principles and major programs were decomposed into more than 20 special research subjects on substation and line engineering, corresponding to the key technology development subjects of UHV. The research achievements were combined with the specified application requirements and converted into further technical design principles. Take the design of the UHV fitting as an example: first, based on theoretical research and corona characteristic testing, the calculation method and parameters of electric field strength on the surface of the bracket was determined. Then, a pertinent study about system integration was conducted, involving concerns of altitude, air humidity, wind speed, ice covering, seismic resistance, difficulty in manufacturing the bracket, and the difficulty of construction and installation. These studies helped in the selection of the materials for the bracket and in the design of an appropriate structure so as to perfectly control the electromagnetic environment.

Equipment

In addition to computer simulation, a range of tests were conducted for the developed equipment, including unit tests, key structure model tests, margin tests, and other special tests. Tests of connecting to the power grids of 500 kV and 750 kV were also implemented to further understand the typical characteristics of UHV structures and materials within strong electromagnetic fields, and to test new structures, materials, and designs.

Construction and Installation

Special research was conducted on the completion acceptance procedure, debugging scheme, and tests of (transmission) line parameters. After several reviews and examinations with the committee and its specialists, the scheme and procedure were eventually determined and implemented to examine the performance of the UHV system and equipment.

Taking the development of the UHV transformer as an example:

- Step 1: State Grid organized first-class experts in comprehensive domains to conduct joint research and propose technical standard systems and specifications, as well as to determine overall technical solutions and principles of engineering design; determined its suppliers by using government-approved procurement methods.
- Step 2: Shenyang Transformer Group Co., Ltd, Xidian Transformer Co., Ltd, and Baoding Tianwei Baobian Electric Co., Ltd independently conducted the engineering design.
- Step 3: Trusted third-party organizations conducted independent verification of the engineering designs (for example, VEI, Zabro Thermal Transformer Research Institute, CESI, KEMA, and Weidmann).
- Step 4: State Grid organized a joint review of the engineering designs for the decisive selection.
- Step 5: State Grid organized joint research to optimize the selected design.
- Step 6: The three transformer firms manufactured the prototype independently and worked to solve any major problems that arose at this stage.
- Step 7: Quality control of the mass production throughout the entire process (integrating the solutions and experiences of the three transformer manufacturers).

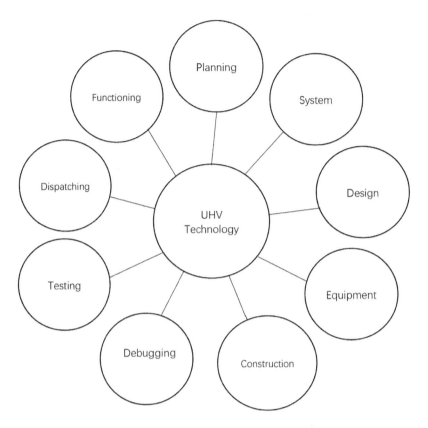

Figure 3.3   The ecosystem of UHV AC Power Transmission

- Step 8: Transportation, installation, testing, debugging, operation, and experience summarization.

3.5   UHV'S SUCCESS IN USER-DRIVEN INNOVATION

By the end of 2017, UHV was transmitting more than 100 billion kWh of hydropower from Southwest to East China annually, and the cumulative delivery had exceeded 550 billion kWh, saving energy costs of more than 50 billion RMB every year. With UHV technology, 19 West–East Power Transmission Projects have been completed in China. The cumulative transmission capacity of these projects has reached 1.2 trillion kWh, and the line length has exceeded 25 000 km. By 2035, more than 80 percent of the clean energy in China will be transmitted with UHV.

The UHV AC Transmission Project has largely promoted the upgrade and leapfrogging development of China's power technology and electrical equipment manufacturing industries. The currently running domestic or foreign systems indicate the good performance of the UHV transmission and transformation system, and the reliability of the relevant equipment. The success of UHV innovation, which has led to "China creating" and "China leading" in electric power technology and equipment manufacturing, relies largely on four crucial factors, explained in the following subsections.

The Synergy of "1+1 > 2"

The UHV project lasted four years, employed thousands of scientists and engineers for R&D and nearly 50 000 people for construction, and organized thousands of academic seminars. All of these activities were led, planned, organized, and financially supported by State Grid, reflecting its outstanding capabilities of coordination in the mega-infrastructure project. In such a large-scale and complex process within a limited time period, it is impossible to succeed without synergy among various complementary and interdependent ecosystem actors. Furthermore, given the many innovation subprojects required for the final value creation, synergy played an even more important role. To a great extent, the project-based, demand-driven, expert-consulted, and process-controlled model developed during this project facilitated such synergy.

A Value Co-creation Process

Despite State Grid's monopolistic position as China's major corporation of power transmission and supply, it still is trying to create more value with groundbreaking innovations. First, the innovation (UHV) fits the long-term interests of the enterprise. Second, the innovation greatly helps to resolve the dilemma of state energy production and usage, as well as the problem of power consumption increase. Third, State Grid gathered and leveraged key resources and capacities in research, manufacture, design, testing, construction, and operation, aiming to break the technological barriers between upstream and downstream enterprises along the industrial chain, to strengthen the cooperation on generic technology research, and to create synergy for innovation based on value exchange, specific requirements, and well-matched cooperation. This, in turn, enhanced the innovation capability and productivity of every ecosystem actor and thus of the entire system. Fourth, the innovation also contributes to local economic development and, at the same time, pollution control and environmental protection.

User-Led Collaborative Innovation

In the UHV project, although State Grid played the leading role, proposing plans and targets and organizing forces and resources, it was also the end-user, since the developed technology had to be useful for improving the efficiency of State Grid's core business of power transmission. Meanwhile, all of the collaborating companies constituting State Grid were users for each other and widely practiced producer–user collaboration. To a great extent, the UHV development was based on a complex producer–user collaborative innovation ecosystem.

Management of the Collaborative Innovation

First, based on the users' demands, a process of demand-oriented basic research, engineering design, equipment development, testing, system integration, and engineering demonstration was adopted. A number of key national projects were approved, based on in-depth research on domestic and foreign technologies, on the technical demands of UHV transmission, and on the 180 research subjects constituting the key technology research framework. This greatly improved the efficiency of the entire innovation system. Second, the cooperative innovation scheme of supply chain management facilitating divergent suppliers' cooperation was initiated to allow for the complex integrative innovation. Third, cooperative management also was implemented for controlling quality and risk, motivating talents, and developing the appropriate culture.

Before the above-mentioned three factors, national guidance and policies for scientific and technological projects, financial support, and tax reduction and exemption also played indispensable roles in enabling the collaborative innovation among various actors.

The Limitations of UHV Innovation

Indeed, the UHV project had limitations, as well. First, administrative resources of the government and resources of the (former) Ministry of Electric Power Industry (abolished in 1998) were deeply involved in the UHV project. Given that a large number of participating companies were public research institutes and equipment enterprises under the command of the (former) Ministry of Electric Power Industry, the achievement of collaborative innovation and the innovation ecosystem obviously displayed the imprint of government intervention, and thus it can hardly be argued that the project was coordinated through market mechanisms.

Second, the success of SOEs' innovation often depends on their capability of controlling the market. It is usually difficult for SOEs to successfully innovate in industries that are highly competitive. For example, regarding the mobile telecommunications industry, in Chapter 4, we will show that companies such as China Mobile and Datang Telecom (with TD-SCDMA) were not as successful as expected due to the fierce competition based on three different telecommunications standards in the market. Yet in the field of UHV transmission, State Grid had the monopolistic position that helped it to comprehensively plan and operate the mega-project as the leader and user.

REFERENCES

Adner, R., and Kapoor, R. (2010). Value creation in innovation ecosystems: How the structure of technological interdependence affects firm performance in new technology generations. *Strategic Management Journal, 31*(3), 306–333.

Autio, E., and Thomas, L. (2014). Innovation ecosystem: Implications for innovation management. In M. Dodgson, D.M. Gann, and N. Phillips (eds), *The Oxford Handbook of Innovation Management* (pp. 204–288). Oxford: Oxford University Press.

Bengtsson, M., and Kock, S. (2000). Coopetition in business networks – to cooperate and compete simultaneously. *Industrial Marketing Management, 29*(5), 411–426.

Brandenburger, A.M., and Nalebuff, B.J. (1996). *Co-opetition: A Revolution Mindset that Combines Competition and Cooperation.* New York: Bantam Doubleday Dell Publishing Group.

Cusumano, M.A., and Gawer, A. (2002). The elements of platform leadership. *MIT Sloan Management Review, 43*(3), 51.

Gawer, A., and Cusumano, M.A. (2002). *Platform Leadership: How Intel, Microsoft, and Cisco Drive Industry Innovation.* Boston, MA: Harvard Business School Press.

Hearn, G., and Pace, C. (2006). Value-creating ecologies: Understanding next generation business systems. *Foresight, 8*(1), 55–65.

Iansiti, M., and Levien, R. (2004). *The Keystone Advantage: What the New Dynamics of Business Ecosystems Mean for Strategy, Innovation, and Sustainability,* Boston, MA: Harvard Business School Press.

Kapoor, R., and Lee, J.M. (2013). Coordinating and competing in ecosystems: How organizational forms shape new technology investments. *Strategic Management Journal, 34*(3), 274–296.

Lettl, C., Herstatt, C., and Gemuenden, H.G. (2006). Users' contributions to radical innovation: Evidence from four cases in the field of medical equipment technology. *R&D Management, 36*(3), 251–272.

Moore, J.F. (1993). Predators and prey: A new ecology of competition. *Harvard Business Review, 71*(3), 75–86.

Teece, D.J. (2007). Explicating dynamic capabilities: The nature and microfoundations of (sustainable) enterprise performance. *Strategic Management Journal, 28*(13), 1319–1350.

Von Hippel, E. (1976). The dominant role of users in the scientific instrument innovation process. *Research Policy, 5*(3), 212–239.

Von Hippel, E. (1986). Lead users: A source of novel product concepts. *Management Science, 32*(7), 791–805.

Von Hippel, E. (2005). Democratizing innovation: The evolving phenomenon of user innovation. *Journal für Betriebswirtschaft, 55*(1), 63–78.

4. TD-SCDMA, LTE-TDD, and China Mobile: catch-up and innovation in the Chinese telecommunications industry

4.1 INTRODUCTION

Before the 1980s, the telecommunications industry in China was dominated by many state-owned enterprises (SOEs), and they focused mainly on fixed phone handsets and manufacturing some components. Due to China's market liberalization reform and open-door policy since the late 1970s, foreign companies began to enter in the mid-1980s, bringing advanced technology such as digital phone switches and wireless communication. Facing rapidly increasing demand that needed to be met through diversified technological innovations, Chinese SOEs pursued large-scale technology imports. At the same time, the transformation of many SOEs into private enterprises and the emergence of joint ventures between domestic and foreign enterprises or wholly owned affiliates of foreign multinationals started to challenge, and even take over, the SOEs' dominant position. With the prosperous development of firms with different ownership structures and specialties, the Chinese telecom equipment industry has become one of the fastest-growing industries, both domestically and globally, since the 1980s.

Thirty years later, China has become a key player in the global telecommunications arena. In recent years, along with the rising 5G era, we have witnessed private firms such as Huawei and ZTE becoming the global lead developers and suppliers. This achievement also indicates the success of indigenous innovation and the catch-up within the Chinese telecommunications industry.

There are different models of catching up. Based on Korea's experiences, Kim (1997) used Utterback and Abernathy's innovation model to identify how the innovation process in a country that is a latecomer differs from that of a developed country. Rather than being limited in the product–process innovation analysis suggested by the Utterback and Abernathy model, Kim proposes a three-stage model for latecomers. The first stage is the acquisition of mature technology from developed countries, through which domestic firms learn production technology. Second, the firms acquire and cultivate process development and product design capabilities. Finally, in the third stage, domestic firms carry out research and development (R&D) activities with originality, thereby developing their own product innovation capabilities. Kim (1997) also argues that process innovation precedes product innovation, and uses the term "reversed innovation process" to highlight this feature.

Lee and Lim (2001) further identify three patterns of catching-up based on the Korean experience: (1) path-following; (2) stage-skipping; and (3) path-creating. Among the three patterns, stage-skipping and path-creating are characterized as "leapfrogging." Path-following means that the companies will follow what the innovative companies did before in successive stages, but in a more efficient way. In the stage-skipping pattern, exemplified by Hyundai's technological development, the latecomer can skip some of the stages that the leading firms have gone through and can strategically adopt the trends of these firms. Path-creating firms, rather than following precisely what the innovative firms did before, develop their own technology to narrow the gap with the leading companies. The development of the CDMA cellular phone system in Korea exemplifies the path-creating pattern.

Recent studies on catching-up have centered on the concept of windows of opportunity. Lee and Malerba (2017) have proposed that there are three types of windows of opportunity: technological, demand, and institutional and public policy. In the traditional steel industry, technological windows of opportunity can be opened through the generation of new technologies, such as the rise of the basic oxygen furnace (Lee and Malerba, 2017). Windows of opportunity also emerge along with the evolution of market demand and consumers' preferences (Tripsas, 2008; Xiong et al., 2017). For instance, the prosperous development of e-commerce in China and the associated business-model innovation in digital finance and logistics are associated with the windows of opportunity in terms of market or demand, rather than with the ones for technology.

In this chapter, in the context of the innovation ecosystem, we examine the catch-up and leapfrogging of the Chinese telecommunications industry through the lens of grasping the technological and market windows of opportunity. Our illustration will focus on a lead firm: China Mobile, which played a prominent role as lead user and operator in the innovation ecosystem and catch-up process of the Chinese telecommunications industry.

For this case, we surveyed the middle managers in China Mobile's technology department in August 2014. We carried out semi-structured interviews with the deputy general R&D manager on the company's 3G and 4G research and development on June 6, 2014. We also interviewed China Mobile's general managers for their technology department on September 1, 2014. In addition, we collected many of the firm's internal and published reports.

4.2   PATH-FOLLOWING CATCH-UP IN GSM AND CDMA

Market Knowledge and Opportunity

In 1987, China began to deploy the wireless phone system (1G), a variant of 900 MHz TACS (analogue technology). The main equipment providers were Motorola and Ericsson. By 1995, there were 3.5 million users (Mobile Telecommunication Research Team, 1997).

In 1994, the Chinese government introduced GSM (the European digital 2G technology), a newer-generation technology and standard that gradually replaced the TACS system. GSM had accumulated 0.15 million users by the end of 1995, while a year later, the user number grew to about 1 million (Mobile Telecommunication Research Team, 1997). Since 1997, the sales of GSM phones have shown rapid and steady growth.

The 1G and subsequent 2G markets were initially opened and controlled by multinational corporations (MNCs). Motorola entered China in 1987, with an office in Beijing, and in 1992, it set up a wholly owned manufacturing site in Tianjin. Motorola had invested 28.5 billion RMB in China by the end of 2000. Through its large-volume investment in the Chinese sector of information and communication technologies (ICT), Motorola became the largest foreign manufacturer in the sector, and the Chinese market became the largest non-United States (US) market for Motorola. Ericsson opened its first office in Beijing in 1985, and in 1992, a joint venture with China Potevio (Putian) was set up (Yueh, 2011). Nokia, the world market leader in mobile phones and terminals in the late 1990s and early 2000s, opened an office in Beijing as early as 1985. The active involvement of world-leading MNCs in the 2G era brought advanced technologies to the Chinese ICT sector and triggered the boom of market demand. Yet, it is clear that the 2G equipment market (infrastructure and terminals) was dominated by Motorola, Nokia, Ericsson, Siemens, Lucent, and Northern Telecom.

Technological Opportunity and the Role of Government

Compared to the digital switches for the fixed-line networks, GSM infrastructure was a more closed technological system with its core technologies protected by patents. Due to the barriers to the core technology, the local operators became locked in to the system dominated by the foreign MNCs.

However, outside the closed system, opportunities for domestic companies' growth emerged, which kicked off a technological and commercial battle between Chinese domestic firms and MNCs. Chinese equipment manufacturers sensed an open window of opportunity to enter the 3G era: that is, the US CDMA system, developed by Qualcomm in San Diego, California in the mid- to late 1990s. CDMA was considered a potential lever to break the GSM monopoly in China. Accordingly, two private enterprises, Huawei and ZTE, headquartered in Shenzhen, a South China city regarded as a pioneer and the engine of innovation and the economic boom, started to dedicate huge resources to the research and development of CDMA technology.

Together with Huawei's and ZTE's efforts as CDMA suppliers, the government strategically promoted the CDMA system to break the GSM monopoly through the establishment of an SOE, China Unicom, as the unique CDMA operator in 1999. Although China is following the CDMA development path of developed countries such as the US and Korea, foreign MNCs still control some core technologies. Therefore, the government imposed the investment policy of "exchange market with technology," which mandated that in the bidding process for national or SOE projects, such as China Unicom's CDMA project, foreign investors could participate only via joint ventures with Chinese firms.

The volume and growth potential of the Chinese market leveraged technological opportunities for domestic firms. Facing governmental pressure, and attracted by the Chinese market, the US CDMA leader Qualcomm began to license its CDMA technologies to Huawei, ZTE, and Datang, such as base stations, switches, and handsets; that is, the entire portfolio of technologies required to build a full working CDMA-based system. With the foreign technology and their own R&D efforts, in 2001, domestic firms such as Huawei and ZTE entered the bidding process to be the equipment suppliers for China Unicom. However, the foreign MNCs, such as Motorola, which were the pioneers in CDMA technology and related products, got the biggest slice of the pie, leaving domestic firms such as ZTE only a small piece. This forced Huawei to go abroad. Based on their constant efforts in CDMA, however, Huawei and ZTE later became members of the W-CDMA club in 3G technologies, as well as increasingly strong players in the GSM infrastructure market.

Knowledge Accumulation and Alliance Strategy

Motorola by then had a wide network of horizontal and vertical linkages with more than 700 local Chinese companies. This resulted in significant knowledge spillovers, especially in areas such as logistics, quality control, and standardization.

Employee turnover is generally an important mechanism for knowledge transfer. A lot of talented scientific and engineering experts in the Chinese labor market were hired by the MNCs. From an interview with the chief technology officer (CTO) of Beijing Capital Telecommunication, an affiliate of China Potevio (also the parent company of a joint venture with Nokia in Beijing), we learned that Capital Telecommunication was the first Chinese company in the mobile phone industry. Its employees acquired rich industrial knowledge through their former work experience in the joint venture with Nokia. However, as an SOE with a strong political imprint, Capital Telecommunication lacked the incentives to utilize the talents of its employees and leverage the potential of their rich knowledge for further innovation, leading to their engineers switching to Huawei, ZTE, and other private Chinese companies. This also indicated that most of the SOEs in the 1990s and early 2000s unwittingly became large training schools for private companies' potential talent.[1]

An interesting question is how domestic Chinese companies were able to enter and catch up in the wireless equipment market at such a fast pace. First, domestic telecommunications pioneers Huawei and ZTE continuously upgraded their technologies through heavy investment in R&D and human resources. Huawei has the highest R&D capacity in the Chinese ICT industry, and strategically targeted 3G technology earlier than other domestic companies. Since its establishment, Huawei has steadily been investing 10–15 percent of its annual sales in R&D, even during the financial crisis period.

Second, both Huawei and ZTE established alliances with foreign companies and utilized the alliance opportunities to learn and absorb the advanced technology. For instance, Huawei created a joint digital signal processing (DSP) lab with Texas Instruments to develop DSP products (that is, chipsets for mobile phones), a communication system lab with Motorola, and a joint lab with Lucent and Sun. Huawei also established partnerships with 3Com and Nortel (within ultra-broadband access solutions). In addition, Huawei has established R&D centers in the US, Sweden, Russia, and India to leverage global knowledge resources and business opportunities. The firm's largest overseas R&D center, located in Bangalore, India, focuses on software development. In 2006, the center had more than 800 engineers.[2]

4.3   INNOVATION ECOSYSTEM FOR TD-SCDMA

As described earlier, the development of 2G telecommunications in China relied mainly on foreign technology. While entering the 3G era, the Chinese government realized that this could be a good opportunity for the Chinese tel-

---

[1]   Based an interview with Mr Lai, former CTO of Beijing Capital Telecommunication, in 2006.
[2]   Based on an interview on April 16, 2006 in Huawei.

ecommunications industry not only to catch up, but also to leapfrog, as the 3G technology was also new to the MNCs from developed economies.

In 2006, the central government enacted a national innovation policy – the National Medium- and Long-Term Program for Science and Technology (S&T) Development (2006–2020) – highlighting indigenous innovation as a vital mechanism and strategy. The national strategic focus and guidance considerably boosted the development of 3G technology. To facilitate the national S&T plan and the indigenous innovation strategy, the Chinese government also played an important role by introducing the new 3G technology to Chinese firms through mobilizing various resources and initiating a brand new industrial innovation ecosystem for 3G. That is to say, not only were the technology developers and suppliers involved, but also the users as well as supply chain and infrastructure were included in the innovation ecosystem for synergy creation and the realization of 3G. Within the innovation ecosystem of 3G technology and technical standards, Chinese SOEs such as China Mobile played an indispensable role in the innovation ecosystem as a lead user of 3G technology and as a service provider.

The Innovation Ecosystem of China Mobile

As a lead telecommunications service provider, China Mobile has abundant network resources to serve a huge number of customers and to sustain its competitive advantages in China. Yet, in the era of rapid development of information and communication technology and the increasing popularity of mobile Internet applications, as an SOE it is obliged to increase investment in technological innovation to catch up with global competitors and incorporate more-advanced ICTs into its services. China Mobile's innovation ecosystem involves three aspects: outcome, component, as well as organization and decision-making (Figure 4.1).

The outcome of China Mobile's innovation ecosystem consists of four parts: products and services that reflect the distinctive features of China Mobile; standards and specifications, especially network protocols and technical standards filling the gaps in this industry; patents and software copyrights that are indispensable for the company to maintain its competitive advantages; and research publications that share innovation achievements and intermediate results with its peers.

Five components are critical to China Mobile's innovation ecosystem: (1) strategy formulation and market research; (2) operation network development; (3) platform development; (4) terminal development; and (5) device testing and certification.

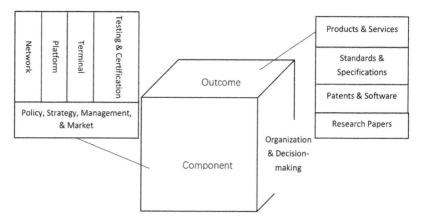

Figure 4.1   China Mobile's innovation ecosystem

Strategy Formulation and Market Research

China Mobile, as a 3G user, formulated its development strategy according to its market investigations which revealed rising and unfulfilled demands in divergent customer segments in the Chinese telecommunications market. In order to maintain its strategy consistency, China Mobile dynamically adjusted its decisions and actions according to market changes and new technological developments. In addition, as an SOE that both undertakes strategic missions for the government and responds to market competition, China Mobile has been striving for the alignment between political and market pressures.

Operation Network Development

To ensure that the operationalization of innovation projects is efficient, operation network development is essential to an innovation ecosystem. The development of an operation network requires an effective and cost-saving working mechanism. Essentially, a hierarchical network structure involves multiple actors, and an agreed technical protocol and operation scheme.

Platform Development

With the development of new technologies such as mobile Internet, big data, and cloud computing, the competition between enterprises or single products in the telecommunications industry is evolving into a competition among platforms. A platform is regarded as an important tool for linking external complementary resources that enterprises need in order to carry out complex innovation activities and, thus, enhance their competitive advantages.

Terminal Development

Competition among telecom operators in the era of the mobile Internet is eventually based on increasing and retaining customers; in particular, increasing and improving the customization of terminals. Due to the consistency of fixed network access and physical location, it is not easy for fixed Internet users to change operators; which, in turn, leads to reliance on the familiar operator. While that is not a problem for mobile Internet users, it is crucial that the company continuously innovates to retain customers and remain competitive. In the mobile Internet era, smartphones are the primary terminals via which customized and specialized services are provided. Indeed, China Mobile has been investing heavily in the development of customized smartphones and applications.

Device Testing and Certification

The huge telecommunications network operated by different enterprises is composed of various information systems for network operation and management, which is an important feature that distinguishes the modern telecommunications network from the traditional one. With the transformation of China Mobile, new businesses are constantly introduced, and the customer services in various market segments are deepened. All of these require particular network equipment with divergent but compatible software, and even particular modes of information transmission. Innovation, by its very nature, is a value-creation process incorporating many interdependent value-adding activities. For instance, while the new ICT services require development of new devices, for network security and creation of the new services, it is crucial to develop better methods and equipment for testing and certification.

Apparently, an innovation ecosystem that leads to prosperous outcomes requires an effective organization and a decision-making structure that enables the addition of the value of each component. Each individual component should have a clear and specific function in the innovation ecosystem, while at the same time, different components should be aligned according to their complementarities in objectives and functions. Hence, the interdependency among ecosystem components and the dynamic interactions among them facilitate achieving the common value proposition of the innovation ecosystem and its benign culture and environment. The organization and decision-making structure of China Mobile for technological innovation is presented in Figure 4.2.

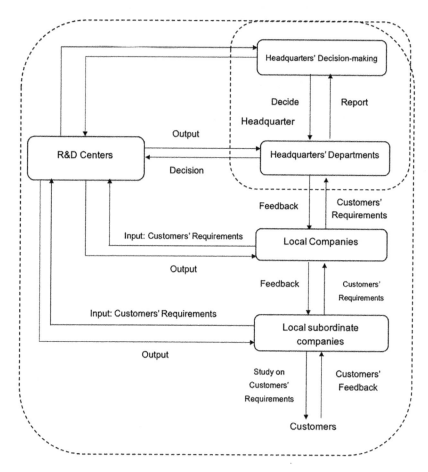

*Figure 4.2   China Mobile's organization and decision-making process
              for technological innovation projects*

Within China Mobile's headquarters, several independent departments oversee
the portfolio of innovation projects; these technological departments follow
the latest global technological trends. Other departments at China Mobile
collect information regarding market trends and customers' major demands.
After analysis, the relevant pieces of technological and market information are
synthesized and submitted to the decision-making board, which develops an
overall strategy for China Mobile's innovation.

China Mobile also has a network of front-line business units – that is, local
branches and subsidiaries all over China – undertaking network construction

and maintenance, as well as providing various services for customers. Due to the proximity to the market and customers, these units usually have a better understanding of the market dynamics and the diversified customer needs, such as the demand for new mobile phone applications and requirements for performance improvement of the current operation network. The fulfillment of market demand usually is not a unidimensional activity; rather, it involves the complex activities of network management, monitoring and maintenance, business management, and accounting systems.

In order to better utilize R&D resources and facilities – such as talent, high-level experimental and testing equipment, and laboratories – China Mobile runs R&D in a centralized mode. Based on strategic guidance from headquarters and front-line market information reported from local business units, the R&D centers organize and carry out projects that consider both technological advancement and market needs.

In 2008, China's Ministry of Industry and Information Technology (MIIT) granted exclusive 3G licenses to a limited number of domestic SOEs. And the issuing of 3G licenses triggered a series of large-scale mergers and acquisitions: China Telecom acquired the CDMA network from China Unicom; China Unicom merged with China Netcom and became the new China Unicom; the basic telecommunications service of China Netcom merged into China Telecom; and China Railcom merged into China Mobile. During this wave of business reconfiguration, six operators merged into three: China Mobile, China Telecom, and China Unicom. Each of them obtained a 3G license and adopted one of the 3G technical standards; together, they formed the "tripartite" structure of the Chinese telecommunications industry.

Collaborative Innovation for TD-SCDMA

To implement the innovation ecosystem approach, the key action is collaborative innovation. The history of the introduction and development of 1G and 2G in China shows that China, including SOEs such as China Mobile, was a latecomer in information communication technologies. In the 2G era, GSM technology was imported, and foreign MNCs such as Nokia, Motorola, and Ericsson were the main equipment suppliers. By the end of the 1990s, 3G communication technology started to prevail worldwide, and the Chinese government began to consider catching up through developing independent technical standards.

Government-affiliated research institutes, mainly Datang, played a proactive role in initiating innovation in the Chinese telecommunications industry through technological development and knowledge accumulation and learning. In April 1997, the International Telecommunication Union (ITU) issued a letter to the world to collect technical specifications for 3G wireless transmission. In response to this letter, the Chinese government took the opportunity to gather relevant information and knowledge and, in July 1997, established the China 3G Wireless Transmission Technology Assessment and Coordination Group, under the leadership of the (former) Ministry of Posts and Telecommunications, to urgently collect related technical materials from universities, research institutes, and enterprises across China.

The China Academy of Telecommunications Technology (CATT), affiliated with the (former) Ministry of Posts and Telecommunications, developed and proposed the technical standards and scheme of TD-SCDMA. On June 30, 1998, the TD-SCDMA proposal was submitted to the ITU. On May 5, 2000, TD-SCDMA was officially approved as one of the 3G international standards at the ITU Turkish Congress. It was the first Chinese telecommunications system technical standard in history to be recognized by the ITU, and at the global level.

However, the Chinese government seemed not to favor the TD-SCDMA at the beginning. By March 2002, the Chinese government still had not confirmed that TD-SCDMA was the standard for China's mobile communications. Nor had it allocated the corresponding frequency bands to launch TD-SCDMA. Nevertheless, Chinese and foreign enterprises had begun to cooperate with each other to further develop TD-SCDMA-related technologies and to discuss commercial launch of the new standard. For example, the TD-SCDMA Technology Forum, co-sponsored by China Mobile, China Telecom, China Unicom, Datang Telecom, Huawei, Motorola, Nortel, and Siemens, was formally established in Beijing on December 12, 2000. It was dedicated to deploying TD-SCDMA and promoting related technological innovations.

In 2001, Datang Telecom cooperated closely with Siemens and finally developed a base station and test terminal based on the TD-SCDMA standard. In April of the same year, the first demonstration of global calling based on TD-SCDMA was organized, and in July, the image transmission from the terminal to the base station was completed. On February 3, 2002, together with Siemens, Datang Telecom conducted the first public demonstration of outdoor mobile voice and image transmission based on the TD-SCDMA system. In the demonstration, TD-SCDMA base station had a coverage radius of 15 km and achieved clear voice and image communication at a movement speed of 70 km/h.

At the stage of commercialization of TD-SCDMA, the government initiated the industrial regulations and the formation of industrial alliances involving the key stakeholders, and it played a key role in promoting the stakeholders' cooperation for the innovation. On October 23, 2002, the Ministry of Industry and Information Technology (MIIT) promulgated the 3G Wireless Spectrum Planning Scheme. Accordingly, four symmetrical FDD bands with a frequency of 60 MHz*2 were reserved for WCDMA and CDMA2000, while 155 MHz asymmetrical TDD bands were reserved for TD-SCDMA.

Preferential governmental policies enabled TD-SCDMA to gain political advantage. On October 30, initiated by the (former) National Development Planning Commission, the MIIT and the Ministry of Science and Technology (MST), eight major domestic telecom enterprises – Datang Telecom, Guangzhou South High-Tech, Holley, Huawei, Lenovo, ZTE, CEC, and China Potevio – established the TD-SCDMA Industry Alliance (TDIA) (Zhan and Tan, 2010). In December 2003, the MIIT, the National Development and Reform Commission (NDRC), and the MST jointly funded the TDIA with 700 million RMB. At the end of February 2004, the NDRC approved the research, development, and industrialization project of TD-SCDMA, which was launched in the same year. TD-SCDMA received further governmental support for promoting independent innovation, as proposed by the government in its medium- and long-term science and technology development plan for 2006–2020. On January 20, 2006, the MIIT formally approved TD-SCDMA as the technical standard of China's 3G telecommunications industry. In March 2006, China Mobile, China Telecom, and China Netcom set up a trial commercial network of TD-SCDMA in Xiamen, Baoding, and Qingdao, respectively, to conduct large-scale tests.

Despite this progress, during the process of commercializing TD-SCDMA-related products and services there were insufficient collaborative efforts for innovation. The firms had diversified interests. In particular, given the fact that TD-SCDMA lacked competitiveness in its early years, the foreign multinationals tended to promote their own technical standards and products instead, and the domestic companies were not dedicated to the success of TD-SCDMA either.

Nokia

Nokia was initially one of the main forces in the WCDMA camp, possessing complete solutions, and was eager to develop its Chinese market with WCDMA. Nokia preached the advantages of WCDMA technology, such as compatibility with GSM, economies of scale, sufficient suppliers, and technical maturity. So, Nokia was not interested in TD-SCDMA and even rejected the proposal of building dedicated networks for it. Nevertheless, with the development of TD-SCDMA – as well as the fact that competitors such as Siemens, Nortel, Ericsson, and Alcatel were on board – Nokia moved towards the TD-SCDMA camp. In October 2005, Nokia and Potevio set up Puno Mobile Communication Equipment Co., Ltd with registered capital of 300 million RMB. China Potevio and Nokia held 51 percent and 49 percent, respectively, of the company's shares. The total investment eventually reached

900 million RMB, and the joint venture's contract was for 15 years. Puno engaged mainly in the R&D, production, and sales and service of TD-SCDMA products and services. Inherently, the strategic partners' interests were only partially aligned with each other, and they were competing outside the alliance. Namely, Nokia could not devote its full effort to supporting TD-SCDMA since it would compete directly with its WCDMA products.

Huawei

With headquarters located in Shenzhen, one of China's most competitive and innovative cities, Huawei and ZTE are two giants in the Chinese tele-communications market. Among the three major 3G standards – WCDMA, CDMA2000, and TD-SCDMA – Huawei invested heavily in the first two, but only to a limited extent in TD-SCDMA. According to *The Truth of Huawei* (Cheng and Liu, 2005), the CEO, Ren Zhengfei, put one-third of the company's R&D efforts into developing products based on the most dominant 3G standard (WCDMA) at that time; whereas he put rather limited efforts into TD-SCDMA (Gao, 2014). On August 29, 2003, just the second day of the International Summit of TD-SCDMA 2003, Huawei announced a joint venture with Siemens that would launch on March 18, 2005: that is, Dingqiao Communications Co., Ltd. The two parties would spend $100 million to jointly develop products based on the TD-SCDMA standard (Siemens and Huawei held 51 percent and 49 percent of the stock, respectively).

ZTE

Huawei's major domestic competitor, ZTE, also joined the 3G race. By 2002, with the announcement of the plan for a 155M asymmetric frequency band of TD-SCDMA, the market prospect of TD-SCDMA was becoming increasingly clear. ZTE started to proactively develop its products based on TD-SCDMA and made great achievements. At the beginning of 2003, ZTE established the TD-SCDMA product line and invested significantly in developing the TD-SCDMA equipment. At the TD-SCDMA 2005 International Summit in Beijing, ZTE presented a full set of commercial equipment for TD-SCDMA. It also conducted a joint live demonstration of 3G multimedia services with Kaiming, T3G, and Samsung. The Minister of Science and Technology at that time even complimented ZTE for being "well prepared for commercializing TD-SCDMA."

Since the second half of 2002, with increasing support of the Chinese government, more and more domestic and overseas telecommunications equipment manufacturers have joined the TD-SCDMA camp. As shown in Figure 4.3, by June 2006, there were more than 40 enterprises in the TD-SCDMA industry chain, including four suppliers of core network equipment, five suppliers of access network equipment, 11 suppliers of terminals, three suppliers of terminal chips, and five suppliers of test instruments. China's TD-SCDMA ecosystem was thereby gradually formed.

TD-SCDMA's Performance

Obviously, operators are the users of mobile communication technologies and play a decisive role in selecting and adopting technical standards and networks. In the early days, China Mobile was not supportive of TD-SCDMA. Many of the company's senior executives explicitly claimed that WCDMA, due to its maturity and stability, was the most suitable technical standard for China Mobile to evolve from the 2G (GSM) to the 3G network between 2002 and 2004. They regarded TD-SCDMA as merely a supplementary solution to WCDMA. In fact, China Mobile did encounter many difficulties in promoting the commercialization and adoption of TD-SCDMA, as well as its derivative technologies.

Although China Mobile was China's largest state-owned operator back then, it had several disadvantages in promoting the use of TD-SCDMA, such as the longer duration of network building, constant updates of the technology, lack of popular applications, little involvement of the international players, and weak terminal (mobile phone) technologies. In comparison, the other two telecommunications giants, China Telecom and China Unicom, outcompeted China Mobile through adopting CDMA2000 and WCDMA, respectively.

In the first quarter of 2010, the total global users of WCDMA and CDMA2000 reached around 698 million, while those of TD-SCDMA were only around 7.7 million,[3] accounting for just 1 percent of the world market. Within the Chinese domestic market, China Unicom and China Telecom were constantly stealing 3G subscribers from China Mobile, which was plagued by problems with TD-SCDMA. The ultimate result was that China Mobile changed its strategic focus to the 4G and devoted its resources to developing LTE-TDD.

Due to limited participation and usage, as well as the development constraints of this technology, TD-SCDMA did not help China Mobile to realize the economies of scale. By the end of September 2010, China Mobile had only 15 million users of TD-SCDMA. By devoting itself to LTE-TDD, the company hoped to win back the high-end users of China Unicom and China Telecom in the 3G business competition. Figure 4.4 shows the number of domestic 3G users of the three Chinese operators in 2013; Figure 4.5 shows

---

[3]   State radio regulation of China: http://www.srrc.org.cn/article2233.aspx.

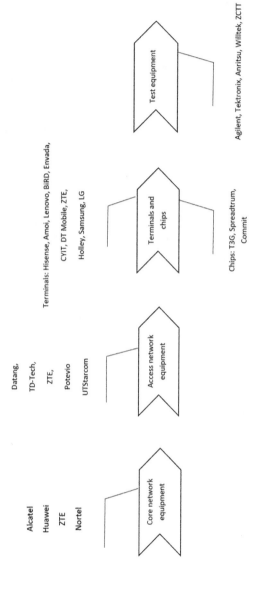

Figure 4.3   Telecom equipment providers in the industrial chain of TD-SCDMA

the proportion of 3G users of the three operators in 2013; and Figure 4.6 shows the comparison of the three 3G operators' technical capabilities. Even though China Mobile was the largest operator in China, and its 3G user number was the highest among the three operators in 2013, its 3G user proportion and base station number were the lowest.

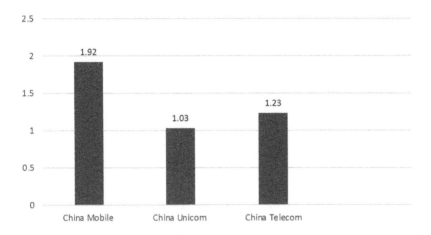

Figure 4.4   *Number of the three Chinese operators' domestic 3G users in 2013 (100 million)*

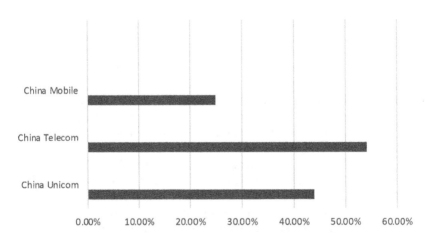

Figure 4.5   *3G user percentage of the three Chinese operators in 2013*

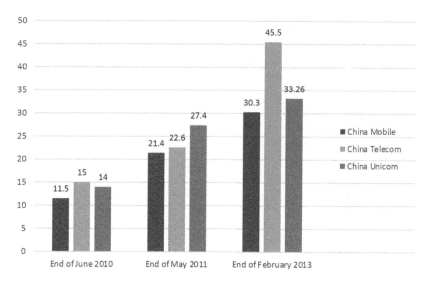

Figure 4.6   3G base stations of the three Chinese operators

4.4   GLOBAL INNOVATION ECOSYSTEM FOR LTE-TDD

The Role of Government

In 2006, the Chinese government formulated and published the National Medium- and Long-Term Program for Science and Technology Development (2006–2020), which underlined the government's intention of supporting indigenous independent innovation. This policy not only encouraged local firms to undertake R&D tasks independently, but also helped to reduce their dependence on foreign technology (Naughton and Segal, 2003; Tsai and Wang, 2011). With the government's support, Chinese enterprises were encouraged to develop key technologies and intellectual property rights, such as TD-SCDMA for the international 3G market (Yu et al., 2012). Despite the fact that TD-SCDMA had been regarded as a model of indigenous innovation, its commercialization was not successful. Due to insufficient technical knowledge and the lack of collaboration among domestic enterprises – as well as the purely domestic-market orientation – the international operators were not interested in collaborating with the domestic firms to develop and commercialize TD-SCDMA-related products and services. Consequently, TD-SCDMA did not become a "superstar" in the 3G era. Considering this, in the Twelfth National Five-Year Plan (2011–2015) the Chinese government deemed that

4G offered an important strategic window of opportunity (Li, 2011). Thus, the central government and China Mobile were both ambitious in developing the 4G technology.

There are two reasons why China Mobile actively promoted 4G, despite its massive investment in 3G TD-SCDMA. First, in the 3G era, China Mobile was designated by the government as a TD-SCDMA operator, even though this technology was not acknowledged by the company's experts and engineers. Second, China Mobile's development was slow, with a decreasing average revenue per user in the 3G era. Meanwhile, its major domestic competitors – China Unicom, which adopted the WCDMA technology, and China Telecom, which used CDMA2000 – had rapidly caught up in terms of market share through their 3G technologies. Under these circumstances, China Mobile had to shift the tide of the telecommunications battle towards the newly emerging 4G.

As one of the 4G technologies and standards, LTE-TDD developed very fast. By January 2014, mobile network operators (MNOs) had deployed 28 LTE-TDD networks in 21 countries. Since then, LTE-TDD services have been provided in many developed and emerging markets, such as Japan, Saudi Arabia, the United States, the United Kingdom, Spain, Australia, South Africa, and the Nordic countries (GSA, 2014). In fact, China Mobile's LTE-TDD has become an important 4G technology on the global stage.

The International Alliance

At that time, LTE-FDD and WiMaX dominated the European and American 4G markets, respectively. With strategic concerns, the Chinese government raised the issue of independently developing a 4G technical standard that aimed to improve the technical capacity and innovation of both Chinese firms and the whole industry. Although the TD-SCDMA standard did not succeed in the 3G era (Parker, 2013), having the world's largest market, and learning from the failures, China Mobile started to create a global ecosystem to avoid the failure of the 3G. China Mobile had been taking a leading role since the beginning of 4G research, and by strategically aligning with other enterprises and with the help of the Chinese government, it proposed and promoted LTE-TDD in both domestic and international markets (Ovum, 2009).

Besides China Mobile, Datang Group was another leading 3G-era company that has also played an important role in the 4G era. In 2004, Datang Group started its own research on LTE-TDD. In 2007, it successfully made the first 4G prototype and conducted relevant tests. At that time, however, the international players did not acknowledge Chinese 4G technology. Many mobile network operators, especially in developed markets, continued to support the development and evolution of LTE-FDD technology (Ovum, 2012). They questioned the implications of the Chinese 4G standard, since the mature and internationally acknowledged technology already existed. China Mobile was, thus, the only operator of LTE-TDD, which in turn forced it to build its own innovative ecosystem in order to survive and develop.

Over time, the advantages of LTE-TDD began to emerge. First, it reduces costs by providing more spectrum segments (Li, 2011). As the LTE-TDD network is compatible with almost all the 2G and 3G applications, it provides great commercial advantages to businesses, allowing them to conduct business in the most profitable and largest market segments. As a result, some international operators, including those who operate LTE-FDD, also purchased the TDD spectrum as a supplement to FDD (TD Industry Alliance, 2013). Second, as the LTE-TDD network is cheaper and faster, it brings more benefits to late-coming operators. Thus, Softbank (Japan), FarEasTone (Taiwan), and operators in South America and South Asia started to adopt it.

China Mobile concluded that insufficient internationalization and compatibility was the main reason for the failure of the TD-SCDMA promotion. Learning lessons from these past failures, China Mobile set a clear goal of internationalizing LTE-TDD, and with a great amount of investment, it initiated an international alliance called TD-LTE Global Technology Initiative (GTI) with Softbank, Vodafone, Bharti Airtel (India), and KT (South Korea) for globally industrializing the TD-LTE (LTE-TDD) and the upcoming 5G technology at the Mobile World Congress (MWC) in 2011. As a result, more international operators chose to participate in the promotion of LTE-TDD, and a snowball effect was created. Eventually, LTE-TDD was recognized globally as a commonly adopted 4G standard.

China Mobile made great efforts to create a new global ecosystem for the TD-LTE. Some key actions are listed below:

- Strategically, since TDD (LTE-TDD) was introduced later than FDD, GTI took TDD as a complementary or ancillary technical standard of FDD to obtain more support across this industry. Meanwhile, low-cost equipment is the primary reason for emerging countries such as China, Russia, and India to use TDD (Ovum, 2012).
- The international technological alliance GTI organized many events such as international conferences, and developed low-cost end-products for its members. China Mobile also held several events to build the TDD global ecosystem, aiming to gain the confidence of international operators. For example, China Mobile and Vodafone have established the first real-time TDD-FDD demonstration network and shown the good performance of TDD in the outdoor environment at the MWC 2011.
- China Mobile was largely devoted to close communication with the operators to gain mutual understanding and consensus over the TDD devel-

opment. Aiming to facilitate the industrialization of the new technology, China Mobile and its partners – including equipment developers, infrastructure builders, and chip developers – conducted many equipment tests.

• Qualcomm became involved. In 2013, a new chip based on LTE was developed by Qualcomm. This chip adapts to seven types of mobile phone networks, including FDD, TDD, and ECDMA. It facilitated producers such as Apple to develop different products to fit different network modes (2G, 3G, or 4G) (Chao, 2013). In this way, a complete mobile communication system for TDD, which consists of chips, terminals, and equipment, was formed. By the end of February 2013, 31 producers had joined this system; these included Samsung, HTC, Apple, and several Chinese mobile phone producers.

• Apple became involved. At first, Apple was reluctant to accept this new standard. But its final decision to join in propelled TDD to a higher level (Yu et al., 2012). Back in 2007, China Mobile attempted to cooperate with Apple and introduce the iPhone to the Chinese market, but the effort failed due to the immature ecosystem of TD-SCDMA. However, the introduction of the LTE-TDD network created a different circumstance, and the iPhone was finally launched in China in 2012. It was a win–win situation: for China Mobile, the most important benefit from the cooperation lay in the branding, enhancing its competitiveness in the high-end market; for Apple, an increase in sales and earnings was the biggest gain.

Afterwards, more and more multinational companies began to adopt TDD, and more than ten of them proposed concrete plans for the industrialization of TDD. Currently, more than 100 operators are the GTI alliance's members, and 76 telecom producers have established partnerships with it. For 4G technology, Chinese companies have adopted a global innovation ecosystem to meet their targets.

China Mobile as a Lead User and Ecosystem Coordinator

China Mobile commenced cooperation with international operators in the early stages of LTE-TDD, jointly promoting this 4G standard. It made efforts to initiate the collaborative innovation along the 4G industrial supply chain and connected upstream component suppliers, including chip manufacturers (for example, Hisilicon and ZTE) and instrument manufacturers (for example, Mi, Huawei, Chuangyuan, Vivo, StarPoint, and Transcom Instruments). They jointly proposed technical solutions, developed components, conducted comprehensive tests, and constantly optimized products. Although China Mobile had more than 200 4G patents, successfully applying them to specific products was rather challenging, given the differences in technical standards among

Table 4.1   Comparison of the three major operators' 4G service by June 2014

	China Mobile	China Telecom	China Unicom
Base stations	410 000	90 000	63 400
Served cities	More than 300	16	16
Terminals	242	28	20

China Mobile and the manufacturers. Hence, China Mobile had to conduct various tests in divergent conditions before maturing and commercializing the TDD, which required a large number of base stations. In a meeting with the mobile phone enterprises, China Mobile released a plan to build 20 000 base stations in 2012 and 200 000 in 2013, based on upgrading the TDS (TD-SCDMA) stations (Xin, 2009). This plan significantly strengthened the mobile phone enterprises' willingness to cooperate with China Mobile.

During the development of 4G, Huawei, ZTE, and Datang Group also made great contributions. For example, Huawei established its open labs for LTE-TDD testing at Xi'an, Shenzhen, and Beijing (Parker, 2013). Considerable financial resources and effort were put into developing the technology, identifying market demand, and developing pertinent products. In addition, since Huawei was devoted to establishing a good company image of being professional and international, for China Mobile, a good partner such as Huawei was very helpful in TDD's internationalization. Another important domestic partner was ZTE. Unlike Huawei, whose target was the high-end users, ZTE won its considerable global market share with its low-priced but high-quality products.

States of 4G and Prospects of 5G

The TD-LTE (LTE-TDD) licenses were issued in December 2013, and China Telecom and China Unicom started their 4G services in 16 cities in June 2014. Comparatively, China Mobile had started its 4G services almost six months earlier, and thus had developed first-mover advantages (Table 4.1).

By the end of June 2014, China Mobile owned more than 410 000 base stations covering more than 300 cities, and it had 242 terminals that support its 4G service. From January to June 2014, 23.41 million total new users adopted China Mobile's services, 59.5 percent of whom chose the 4G service. In spite of the low ratio of 4G users to total users, the average revenue per user (ARPU) of China Mobile was three times more than that of the average. In comparison, China Unicom owned 63 400 base stations, among which 5400 were TD-LTE stations and 58 000 were LTE-FDD stations, covering 16 trial cities; clearly

Table 4.2   *Patents of the six operators (2009–2014)*

Year	NTT DoCoMo	Verizon	Vodafone	China Mobile	China Telecom	China Unicom
2014	386	386	216	181	6	35
2013	1561	578	178	1091	11	458
2012	1612	500	211	858	2	503
2011	1803	567	238	500	56	230
2010	1783	538	335	545	15	175
2009	2370	533	341	935	16	284

far less coverage than that of China Mobile. China Telecom owned 90 000 4G base stations and had 28 terminals that support its 4G service.

As a key indicator of technological innovation, the number of patents largely determines the competitiveness and market shares of telecom operators. The patent numbers of the three domestic operators and three international operators are presented in Table 4.2.

With the success of TD-LTE and the establishment of the global cooperative innovation alliance, China Mobile is now tackling the 5G era. In the global 5G testing summit of the MWC 2017, a joint declaration was issued by China Mobile, AT&T, NTT DOCOMO, Vodafone, Huawei, Ericsson, Intel, ZTE, Nokia, Qualcomm, Keysight, Rhodes & Schwartz, and Datang Group, aiming to promote a global, unified technical standard and to build a global, unified 5G ecosystem (Li, 2017).

At the beginning of 2013, the Chinese government organized an alliance for promoting the development of IMT-2020 (the formal name of 5G). China Mobile was the first to join. In 2014, it launched the development agenda to facilitate the standard formulation, technical verification, industrial chain development, and product improvement. China Mobile partnered with Huawei, Qualcomm, ZTE, Intel, and Ericsson in 2016 and established a joint innovation center for developing the 5G technology. To date, it has more than 42 partners. Further enhancing its international status in the field of 5G, and thus obtaining more international recognition and more partners, China Mobile planned to commercialize the 5G technology in 2019.

LTE-TDD's Success and Open Innovation Ecosystem

LTE-TDD is promoted not only in China, but also in many other countries such as Japan and European and Middle Eastern countries. At the GTI International Industry Summit in 2018, Shang Bing, the Board Chair of China Mobile, mentioned that 111 LTE-TDD commercial networks had been deployed in

58 countries and regions, including 37 LTE-TDD/FDD integrated networks with more than 1.26 billion users worldwide. These numbers reflect the global recognition of LTE-TDD and the open innovation ecosystem's success.

The process of innovation involved not only domestic enterprises, such as China Mobile, Huawei, and ZTE, but also many international companies. Among all of these companies, both domestic and foreign, China Mobile played a leading role. Unlike the development of 3G, which was led by the technology providers, China Mobile played the role of a lead user during the development of 4G, and continuously improved the technology according to the market demand. In retrospect, the development of 3G was burdened with too many missions, which resulted in excessive government intervention and inefficiencies. For example, Datang Group was the developer of the 3G standard which has a limited capacity for industrialization, whereas Huawei and ZTE did not make full use of their advantageous capacities. The functioning of the 3G strategic alliance, formed by the government, was largely fruitless due to ineffectual coordination (Tsai and Wang, 2011). The collaborative innovation in the 3G era was mostly confined to domestic enterprises and failed to enter the international market, while the success of 4G largely relied on international cooperation, even at a very early stage of the technology's emergence.

China Mobile clearly understood that to make LTE-TDD a global 4G standard, it could not depend solely on the government. That explains why China Mobile initiated GTI, trying to work with international partners to promote the development of LTE-TDD. As the most influential organization dedicated to the development of LTE-TDD, GTI has become a crucial player in the global LTE-TDD alliance. As happened in the case of UHV mentioned in Chapter 3, members of the alliance became users of each other's products along the industrial chain. Unlike the UHV case, however, the user pool of telecommunications standards and networks was much more international, as the demand for advanced mobile telecommunications was more universal than the demand for UHV.

REFERENCES

Chao, C. (2013). Market opportunity of China Telecom 3G toward 4G – a social-technical analysis for its future development. Available at SSRN 2259178.

Cheng, D., and Liu, L. (2005), *Truth of Huawei* (in Chinese), Beijing: Dandaizhongguo Press.

Gao, X. (2014). A latecomer's strategy to promote a technology standard: The case of Datang and TD-SCDMA. *Research Policy*, 43(3), 597–607.

GSA (2014). GSA status of the LTE ecosystem report: 1,371 LTE user devices launched by 132 suppliers. Retrieved from: www.gsacom.com/php/access.php4.

Kim, L. (1997). *Imitation to Innovation.* Boston, MA: Harvard Business School Press.

Lee, K., and Lim, C. (2001). Technological regimes, catching-up and leapfrogging: Findings from the Korean industries. *Research Policy*, *30*(3), 459–483.

Lee, K., and Malerba, F. (2017). Catch-up cycles and changes in industrial leadership: Windows of opportunity and responses of firms and countries in the evolution of sectoral systems. *Research Policy*, *46* (2), 338–351.

Li, K. (2011). Why Chinese 4G matters to the rest of the world. *Ericsson Business Review*, *1*, 58–59.

Li, X. (2017). The war of three big operators on 5G. March 10. Accessed October 28, 2020 at http://tech.163.com/17/0310/22/CF6TLLUF00097U7S.html.

Mobile Telecommunication Research Team (1997). Research on innovation strategy of mobile telecommunication industry. State S&T Committee and Ministry of Electronics. Working Report.

Naughton, B., and Segal, A. (2003). China in search of a workable model: Technology development in the new millennium. In W. Keller and R. Samuels (eds), *Crisis and Innovation in Asian Technology* (pp. 160–186). Cambridge: Cambridge University Press.

Ovum (2009). Datang Mobile: A TD-SCDMA leader. London: Ovum.

Ovum (2012). First TDD-LTE smartphone on sale in India. London: Ovum.

Parker, T. (2013). China Mobile commits $6.7B to LTE TDD Capex in 2013. Retrieved from: www.fiercebroadbandwireless.com/story/china-mobile-commits -67b-LTETDDcapex- 2013/2013-03-17.

TD Industry Alliance (2013). *LTE TDD Industry Development Report (2012).*

Tripsas, M. (2008). Customer preference discontinuities: A trigger for radical technological change. *Managerial and Decision Economics*, *29*(2–3), 79–97.

Tsai, C., and Wang, J. (2011). How China institutional changes influence industry development? The case of TD-SCDMA industrialization. Paper presented at the DRUID, Copenhagen Business School, Denmark, June 15–17.

Xin, L. (2009). Smoothing the road to mobile broadband. Retrieved from: http:// wwwen.zte.com.cn/endata/magazine/ztetechnologies/2009year/no11/articles/ 200912/t20091222_178920.html.

Xiong, H., Hu, Y., and Wu, G. (2017). Market trajectory and catching-up evidences from China. Available at SSRN 3287631.

Yu, J., Zhang, Y., and Gao, P. (2012). Examining China's technology policies for wireless broadband infrastructure. *Telecommunications Policy*, *36*(10), 847–857.

Yueh, L. (2011). *Enterprising China: Business, Economic, and Legal Developments since 1979*. Oxford: Oxford University Press.

Zhan, A., and Tan, Z. (2010). Standardisation and innovation in China: TD-SCDMA standard as a case. *International Journal of Technology Management*, *51*(2–4), 453–468.

5. China's high-speed train dream: CSR Group and the state-led innovation ecosystem

The high-speed train is an important symbol of rail transport modernization and has an increasing influence on China's social and economic development. Although in China, the high-speed train project started much later than those in many developed countries – some of which had had high-speed trains for more than 40 years – it took only six years for China to catch up and even leapfrog most developed countries. China's high-speed rail technologies have enabled its electric multiple units (EMUs) to operate over the longest mileage with the fastest running speed in the world. As a giant in China's rail transportation equipment industry, China South Locomotive & Rolling Stock Co., Ltd (CSR Group) established a cooperative innovation ecosystem for indigenous high-speed train development, under the leadership of the Ministry of Railways (MOR) and supported by domestic universities and scientific research institutes. The high-speed train innovation ecosystem was further extended due to the formation of CRRC Corporation Limited, which derived from the merger between CSR Group and China North Locomotive and Rolling Stock Industry Corporation (CNR Group).

The development of the high-speed train is a milestone in China's industrialization and infrastructure construction, as well as an example of China's indigenous innovation capabilities. It also illustrates how the Chinese mode – that is, the whole-national system – works to stimulate groundbreaking innovations in civil industries. We propose here that the development of the high-speed train was the result of a state-led innovation ecosystem. As the project entailed extremely high costs and complexity, only a strong government and an innovation ecosystem with clear vision and guidance could see the high-speed train to completion. For this project, the Ministry of Railways not only played the role of ecosystem leader, but also acted as the user of high-speed train technologies and rolling stock devices, as well as the operator of the high-speed railway.

The material for this chapter mainly comes from the interviews with high-level managers at China South Locomotive & Rolling Stock Co., Ltd in Beijing on June 24, 2014. Additional material is from CSR Group's internal reports and some from published reports.

5.1   CHINA SOUTH LOCOMOTIVE & ROLLING STOCK CORPORATION

China South Locomotive & Rolling Stock Co., Ltd (CSR) was jointly established by the China South Railway Group Company and the Beijing Iron Industry and Trade Corporation on December 28, 2007, approved by the State Council and the State-owned Assets Supervision and Administration Commission (SASAC). The CSR is a large centrally managed (by SASAC) state-owned enterprise (SOE) focusing on railway construction and rolling stock device manufacturing.

Before the establishment of the CSR, many of its subsidiaries belonged to the Ministry of Railways. When the financial crisis swept the world in 2008, the CSR was listed in the Shanghai and Hong Kong stock markets on August 18 and 21, respectively. Before being merged with the China North Locomotive & Rolling Stock Co., Ltd (CNR Group), it had 20 wholly owned and holding subsidiaries with 90 000 employees in 11 provincial districts. Headquartered in Beijing, the CSR engaged mainly in developing, manufacturing, selling, repairing, and leasing railway locomotives, buses, wagons, electric multiple units (EMUs), and urban rail vehicles. It also covered the extended industries of rail transportation equipment, related technical services, consulting, industrial investment and management, as well as the import and export businesses (see Table 5.1).

In 2013, the annual operating income of CSR Group reached 97.89 billion yuan, an increase of 8.21 percent over the previous year's income. The net profit distributable to shareholders of the listed companies reached 4.14 billion yuan, 3.26 percent more than the previous year's profit. The newly signed orders reached 135 billion yuan throughout the year, with an increase rate of 65 percent compared with the previous year. The CSR's new contracts for city rail vehicles made it the global leader, and its products with an elastic component managed to cover all of the European high-speed rail markets. CSR Group's high-end products became popular in the international market and attracted global orders, such as EMU orders from Argentina and Malaysia, diesel multiple unit (DMU) orders from Iraq, and electric locomotive orders from Ethiopia. The value of each of the above-mentioned orders exceeded US$100 million. By the end of 2013, the company's orders in process were valued at approximately 111 billion yuan, a 42 percent increase over the value of 2012's orders.[1]

---

[1]   Data from China South Locomotive Rolling Stock Corporation Annual Report, 2013.

Table 5.1   *The CSR's major products and technologies*

High-speed EMUs	Technical system and technical standard system for high-speed EMUs with independent intellectual property rights. Research, development and manufacture of high-speed EMUs with running speed over 350 km/h. A new generation of high-speed EMUs with independent intellectual property rights. Seriation of high-speed EMUs.
Intercity EMUs	Passenger transports that are suitable for shuttling between cities. New types of rail transit products with different speed grades. New intercity EMUs that are suitable for short inter-station distance, large fluctuation in passenger number, and rapid start-and-stop.
Electric locomotive	Electric locomotives for passenger-dedicated lines and trunk lines: C0-C0 six axles with a load of 21 t; able to reach the speed of 200 km/h. Design platform for passenger electric locomotives to build the B0-B0 four-axle and eight-axle passenger electric locomotives with running speed of 200 km/h.
Diesel–electric locomotive	Manufacture platform for 6000 horsepower diesel–electric AC locomotive. High-power diesel-electric AC locomotive of heavy load freight with axle weight of 30 t.
Wagon	Various types of wagons with load capacity of 80 t, axle weight of 27 t and ordinary running speed of 120 km/h. Wagons for the coal transportation line with load capacity of more than 27 t and running speed of 100 km/h. Special open and hopper wagons with axle weight of 30 t and running speed of 100 km/h for the new cargo line. New double-deck container wagons. Fast container wagons and baggage and parcel express wagons with running speed of 160 km/h. New wagons for transporting commercial automobiles.
Urban rail vehicle	Development platform of the urban rail vehicles with independent intellectual property rights. Urban rail vehicles using different materials with running speed range of 80–120 km/h.
Construction machinery	Developing machinery and key parts of construction, maintenance, repair and rescue in rail transit engineering, and relevant product series. Upgraded tamping vehicles, rail welding vehicles, rail grinding vehicles, catenary inspection vehicles, snow sweeping and deicing vehicles, and track inspection vehicles. Developing comprehensive equipment for construction, testing, and maintenance of high-speed passenger lines and electrified railways. Conducting comprehensive research on localizing and serializing shield tunneling machine and tunnel boring machine for subway and tunnel construction. Developing technological innovation system for specialized, serialized, and standardized machinery.

New energy industry	Wind turbines with power of 2.5MW, 3MW, 5MW, and above. Offshore wind power generator. Developing a range of photovoltaic converter systems with the function of real-time diagnosis and remote monitoring for the large and medium-sized solar power plants and photovoltaic power generators on buildings.
New material industry	Conducting research as well as engineering application of new material development. Developing rubber damping materials, modified engineering plastics, noise-reducing materials, polyurethane resin materials, insulating materials and special coatings, composite materials and membrane separation materials, based on the development of polymer composite technology as well as vibration and noise reduction technology.
New energy automobile	Technical platforms of power system and motor drive system of pure electric vehicles and hybrid electric buses. Developing the technology of lightweight vehicles and the technology of optimizing integration of electric buses.

Before the merger with NSR Group, the CSR had a complete system of independent research and development (R&D), manufacturing, and standard service for railway locomotives, buses, wagons, EMUs, metro vehicles, and their components and parts. The company was equipped with the largest electric locomotive R&D base in China, including a high-speed EMU R&D base with globally leading technology; a leading high-powered diesel locomotive and diesel engine R&D base; and a globally leading R&D and manufacturing base of railway wagons. In addition, the CSR was the largest manufacturer of urban metro vehicles in China. Based on its rail transit technologies, the CSR also developed related products, such as electric automobiles, wind-power generation equipment, auto parts, marine crankshafts and diesel engines, high-powered semiconductor components, and construction machinery.

5.2   CSR GROUP'S HIGH-SPEED TRAIN PROJECT: STATE-LED INNOVATION

Under the unified guidance of the Ministry of Science and Technology and the Ministry of Railways, CSR Group followed the general requirements of the State Council for high-speed train development: to import advanced technology, combine design and production, and build China's top brand. To meet these requirements, the CSR established an innovation ecosystem combining manufacture, research and implementation. The formation and development of the innovation ecosystem could not be viable without strong government support. As shown in Figure 5.1, the technical development of high-speed EMUs went through four stages: introduction and absorption; improvement; comprehensive innovation; and continuous innovation.

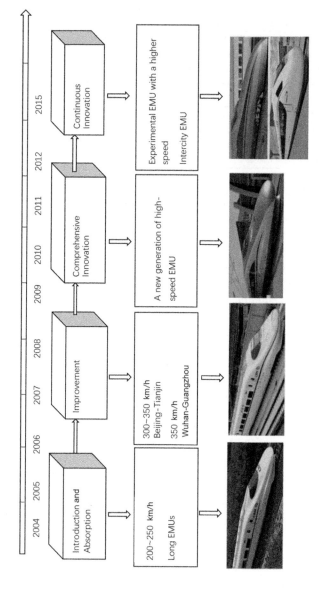

Figure 5.1   The technological stages of the CSR's high-speed train

In August 2004, the Ministry of Railways decided to import the leading international technologies and implement "the sixth railway-speed increase," raising the train speed from 140 km/h to 250 km/h. The Ministry arranged international bidding to import 160 trains with running speeds of 200 km/h, together with all the related technologies, with a budget up to US$12 billion. Attracted by the principle of exchanging market shares with technologies, foreign high-speed train manufacturers entered the Chinese market. Alston (France), Kawasaki Heavy Industries (Japan), and Bombardier (Canada) won the final bid. In November 2005, the Ministry signed a framework agreement with Siemens (Germany), agreeing to spend about US$9 billion to import 60 high-speed trains (300 km/h), together with relevant technical projects. After two rounds of technology import, remarkable progress was realized through re-engineering and absorbing the imported technologies, including original technology development.

In April 2007, the nationwide railway system implemented "the sixth railway-speed increase" and started to use the new train operation diagram. At that point, the high-speed trains started to operate widely. Thus, a series of milestones for the Chinese dream of high-speed trains were achieved.

In February 2008, the Ministry of Railways and the Ministry of Science and Technology agreed on a program to jointly develop and operate a new generation of high-speed trains with a running speed of up to 380 km/h. In August 2008, the first high-speed intercity railway service from Beijing to Tianjin in China started to operate. The intercity railway project and system were based on completely independent intellectual property rights and world-class standards. In December 2009, high-speed railway service from Wuhan to Guangzhou began to operate, with the most advanced and complicated engineering techniques worldwide. In February 2010, the world's first high-speed rail built on collapsible loess, from Zhengzhou to Xi'an, began operations with a running speed of 350 km/h. In April 2010, the high-speed intercity railway service from Shanghai to Nanjing started to operate. In September 2010, during the test run from Hangzhou to Shanghai Hongqiao, the train reached a speed of 416.6 km/h. In December 2010, in a comprehensive test run from Zaozhuang to Bengbu, the new generation of high-speed train (380A) reached a maximum speed of 486.1 km/h, which once again broke the maximum speed record.

The Ministry described the independent innovation of high-speed trains as a three-phase process. In the first phase, through import, digestion, and absorption and re-innovation, the manufacturing system and technology platform of the EMUs with a running speed of 200–250 km/h were developed. More importantly, Chinese manufacturers learned and assimilated the nine key technologies of EMUs. In the second phase, Chinese firms independently developed the high-speed train with a running speed of 350 km/h. Meanwhile, significant breakthroughs were achieved in key technologies for increasing speed, such as wheel-rail dynamics, aerodynamic control, and vehicle body structure. In the third phase, based on a large number of experiments, studies, and test operations, a range of technological innovations were realized, and a new generation of high-speed trains with a running speed of 380 km/h was successfully developed. Moreover, significant breakthroughs were made, including bottleneck technologies in streamlined front, airtightness and strength, and vibration mode (MOST, 2015). From importing foreign technologies to independently developing a world-class domestic high-speed train system, CSR Group took only four years to complete such a remarkable achievement.

On April 18, 2006, 47 high-speed trains manufactured by the CSR were put into operation. The independently developed high-speed trains with running speeds of 300 km/h have been running smoothly on the Beijing–Tianjin intercity railway line. China has also exported several products based on original and integrated innovation to more than 30 countries and regions, including to the high-end market. CSR Group independently manufactured the nine key components of high-speed trains, such as the system, vehicle body, bogie, traction motor, traction transformer, traction converter and traction control, computer-network control, and braking system.

5.3   R&D OF CSR GROUP

Historically, R&D and construction of the railway system played an essential role during the infrastructure establishment and economic recovery of the People's Republic of China (PRC). The Ministry of Railways mostly led the R&D system for railway technology. In 1986, parts of the Ministry spun off and were transformed into a large SOE: China National Railway Locomotive & Rolling Stock Industry Corporation (LORIC), which was further split into two competing SOEs: CSR Group and CNR Group. Though the organization and governance structure have gone through drastic changes over time, the legacy of the rich R&D foundation was inherited by CSR Group and has served as the basis for the state-led innovation ecosystem of the high-speed train.

Founded in 2002, CSR Group had 22 wholly owned and holding subsidiaries in more than ten provincial districts nationwide, with a total of more than 90 000 employees, among whom were two academicians from the Chinese Academy of Engineering (including the only one in the field of rail transit equipment manufacturing in China); nine national-level young and middle-aged experts; 134 government-subsidized experts; 283 professor-level senior engineers; 16 chief technical experts; 98 technical experts; 1726 senior engineers; 231 top talents; and 15 000 engineers and technicians. In 2013, the

CSR applied for 2603 patents, including 1065 invention patents; 1806 were authorized, including 235 invention patents.

A representative subsidiary, CSR Sifang (CSR Qingdao Sifang Co., Ltd) is based in Qingdao, Shandong Province, and specializes in rolling stock manufacturing. As an SOE with backbone technologies in railway and high-speed train design and development, it played a vital role in the national high-speed train project and steadily increased its R&D investment over the years (Table 5.2). Sifang's R&D investment covered more than 5 percent of its annual sales – a relatively large proportion for a manufacturing company – indicating its great emphasis on innovation.

In the early stages of its technological capability development, as shown by Stages I and II in Table 5.2, CSR Sifang had only around 637 technical personnel, including 420 for design and development, 210 technicians and seven project managers. In the later development phases, such as in the CRH380A Project, a large number of external experts were involved, including 68 academicians from Chinese Academy of Engineering, more than 500 professors, and more than 200 researchers, coming from 25 universities, 11 research institutes, and 51 national laboratories and engineering research centers. Eventually, by 2013, CSR Sifang had developed 430 patents, including 20 inventions, 345 utility models and 65 appearance designs relating to the development and manufacturing of high-speed trains (Table 5.3).

Figure 5.2 shows the R&D process of CSR Group. In general, based on comparative analyses and loop verification with simulation, bench test, and line test, the CSR greatly improved the efficacy and accuracy of its technical solutions. Through operational tracking and continuous improvement after product delivery, the safety and reliability within the entire life cycles of its products were improved significantly, which in turn helped with the continuous optimization of its R&D process.

5.4   WHY THE CSR ENGAGED IN DEVELOPING THE HIGH-SPEED TRAIN: A DEMAND-DRIVEN PERSPECTIVE

The CSR's High-Speed Train Project originated primarily from market demand both domestically and internationally. For the domestic market, according to the Medium- and Long-Term Railway Network Plan announced in January 2004, the length of the national railway would reach 95 000 kilometers by 2010, and new railway lines with a length of 19 800 kilometers would be completed within five years, implying the largest demand across the world for high-speed trains, high-power locomotives, and heavy-duty wagons. Meanwhile, China's urban rail transit was also developing very fast. Thirteen cities had reported urban rail construction plans, and 45 lines were planned for

Table 5.2   CSR Sifang's R&D investment (10 000 CNY)

Research project	2006	2007	2008	2009	2010	2011	2012	2013	Total
Stage I: Technology Import and Joint Design									
CRH2A	6 165	4 059	– –	– –	– –	8 793	– –	– –	19 017
Stage II: Digestion Absorption and Integrated Innovation									
CRH2 (250 km/h)	– –	– –	8 468	1 531	– –	– –	– –	– –	9 999
CRH2E	– –	– –	7 852	10 298	– –	– –	– –	– –	18 150
CRH2C (300-350 km/h)	– –	8 789	9 958	15 306	22 571	3 656	2 224	556	63 060
Stage III: Evolution and Comprehensive Innovation									
CRH380A CRH380AL(new front)	– –	– –	– –	7 344	22 800	25 320	22 962	10 798	89 224
Testing EMUs (400 km/h)	– –	– –	– –	– –	– –	5 168	740	– –	5 908
Stage IV: Continuous Innovation and Leadership									
Experimental EMUs with higher speed	– –	– –	– –	– –	6 064	22 682	4 400	1 564	34 710
CRH6 Intercity EMUs	– –	– –	– –	– –	– –	5 852	17 423	7 677	30 952
Total	6 165	12 848	26 278	34 479	51 435	71 471	47 749	20 595	27 1020

Table 5.3   *Patents of CSR Sifang in the field of high-speed EMUs over 2013*

Components	Invention	Utility model	Appearance design	Total
Vehicle body	5	44	7	56
Tooling	6	70		76
Toilet device		9		9
Air conditioning	3	24		27
Train control	1	10		11
Internal assembly	2	112	13	127
Traction motor		4		4
Traction system		2		2
Network control system		10		10
Braking system		8	1	9
Bogie	1	48		49
Assembly	2	4	44	50
Total	20	345	65	430

completion by 2010, achieving 1200 kilometers in total and demanding about 6000 urban rail vehicles.

In the international market, due to the development of new technologies, the international energy conflicts, and the increase in environmental protection awareness, governments worldwide have increasingly favored railway transportation. In addition, many countries in North America, Central Asia, Eastern Europe, Southeast Asia, and other regions started a new round of rail transit equipment renewal, and international rail transit equipment procurement was entering a peak period. In short, the huge domestic and overseas demand has driven the fast development of Chinese high-speed trains, providing considerable values for all parties involved.

Essentially, the technology of high-speed EMUs is a modern high-tech integration, and the high-speed railway system is a typical complex product system, consisting of 140 independent subsystems and more than 40 000 components. As shown in Figure 5.3, it is a multidisciplinary domain, involving technologies of information and communication, power electronics, materials and chemicals, and machinery manufacturing.

In the process of localizing high-speed rail products, additional technological complements were also required. First, the railway system had to adapt to China's operating environments, including divergent geographical

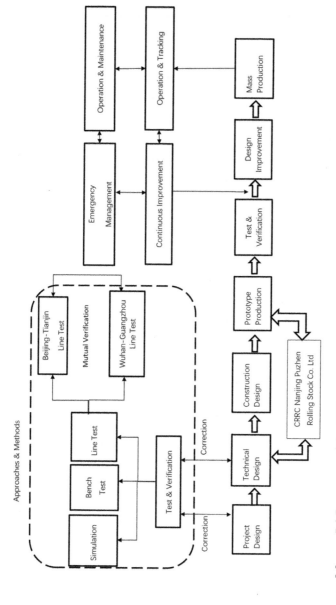

Figure 5.2   R&D process of the CSR

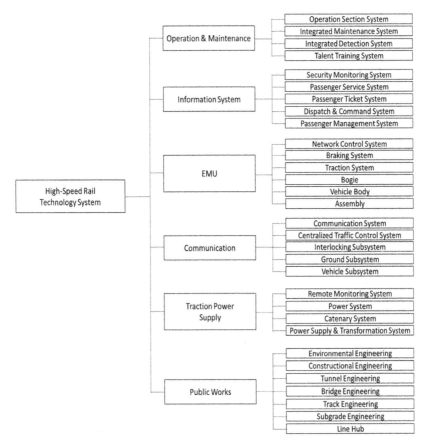

Figure 5.3   Composition of the high-speed rail technology

environments and long-distance, large-capacity, and high-density transportation (Liu et al., 2011). Taking roadbed technology as an example, China has a vast territory with divergent geological and climatic conditions (Liu et al., 2011): the Beijing–Tianjin intercity railroad was built on soft soil, the Wuhan–Guangzhou high-speed railway on karst, and the Zhengzhou–Xi'an high-speed railway on collapsible loess. Therefore, for the high-speed train projects, different roadbed filling technologies were required under various construction contexts, and it was obvious that the foreign technology suppliers from Japan, France, and Germany had never encountered such complicated geological conditions and were unaccustomed to the complex situation in China. Thus, original and indigenous innovations were inevitable, and the demand for high-speed rail transit products in the future will be divergent, ranging, for example, from sand-resistant EMUs to cargo EMUs that can be adapted to passenger lines, and to other products suitable for different environments and conditions.

Second, speed, safety, comfort, and economy are the major demands from most passengers. Meeting the widespread demand for increased speed and decreased travel time can further enhance the market competitiveness of high-speed trains. Yet a speed increase does not imply a simple increase in the power source; rather, a comprehensive consideration of safety performance requiring a range of innovations, such as vehicle body, roadbed, bridge, and track, is of similar or even greater importance. For example, when running speed exceeds 320 km/h, the original rules and relationships between the subsystems will change and need to be redefined. Hence, comprehensive innovation was needed for the entire high-speed train system, such as technical breakthroughs to address a range of issues in systematic couplings (including wheel–rail relation, fluid–solid coupling, and pantograph–contact line relation). Furthermore, technologies were deployed for the interior optimization based on passengers' travel habits and demands. For example, when the CRH380AL model was developed, the CSR conducted a full investigation and analysis of the optimum passenger seats. The ideal ratio of second-class seats to first-class seats and to VIP seats was finally determined to be 20:3:0.5. Personalized areas such as sightseeing areas were also configured, with complete service facilities. In fact, the human–machine interaction theories were well deployed to create a better interior space and environment.

The State Council defined the overall policy of China's high-speed rail industry development as: "import advanced technology, jointly design and produce, and then build Chinese brands," and it approved the Medium- and Long-Term Railway Network Plan and the National Science and Technology Support Plan. In April 2004, the State Council convened a special meeting on the rapid development of China's railway passenger transport and how to modernize rail transit equipment. The meeting resulted in the following plan: the Chinese high-speed rail system would catch up with the technological achievements of Western countries within five years; and the running speed of domestic trains would increase to 350 km/h, which, in turn, would drive a higher level of innovation in the rail transit industry.

Meanwhile, the huge demand in China's market also attracted the attention of internationally renowned rail transit equipment manufacturers such as Bombardier, Siemens, and Alstom. Under the overall guidance of the State Council, these manufacturers tried to enter the Chinese market through technology export. The national policy essentially provided the CSR and other related enterprises with a huge opportunity: to import technologies and then enhance their own independent innovation capabilities, thus achieving catch-up, and perhaps even leapfrogging the global leaders.

The competition in the rail transit equipment market was becoming increasingly fierce, and there were many homogeneous products in China's domestic market. Although the CSR's products had been exported to many countries in Asia, Africa, and South America, low prices were the only means to entering these global markets, as the products' competitiveness was not comparable to that of foreign products at the time due to the lag in technical advancement and reliability. Further, vicious price competition had severely squeezed the profit margin and affected the CSR's sustainable development. Consequently, the CSR had to change its strategy and differentiate its products with technological innovation. On the basis of a systematic analysis of the market environment and its own situation, the CSR realized that, in order to catch up with the world's advanced companies, it had to seize the good opportunities to further develop the domestic market first: starting with learning, digesting, and absorbing foreign advanced technological achievements; then developing a collaborative innovation system to leverage the advantages of partner firms to overcome existing obstacles and achieve independent innovation; and, finally, increasing its global market shares of high-end products.

5.5   THE FUNCTIONING OF THE CSR'S INNOVATION ECOSYSTEM

The CSR put great effort into cultivating and strengthening its independent innovation capabilities. It effectively integrated internal and external innovation resources, built an efficient innovation ecosystem combining industry, academia, and users, and thus greatly shortened the cycle from research and development to production. To convey a comprehensive understanding of the complex product system of the high-speed train, we illustrate the CSR's innovation ecosystem from internal and external angles.

The Internal Innovation Ecosystem

Led by CSR Group, a new cooperative relationship was developed for conducting the high-speed EMUs project, by a number of subordinate enterprises and R&D organizations, including the National Engineering Laboratory of High-Speed Train System Integration, the National Engineering Centre of Converter Technology, five state-accredited corporate technology centers, five postdoctoral workstations, the overseas industrial electric and electronic research and development center, and a number of provincial technical certification centers, as well as industrial technology research centers and key laboratories (Figure 5.4). The R&D on key systems, components, and materials was carried out together to improve the products' quality and performance.

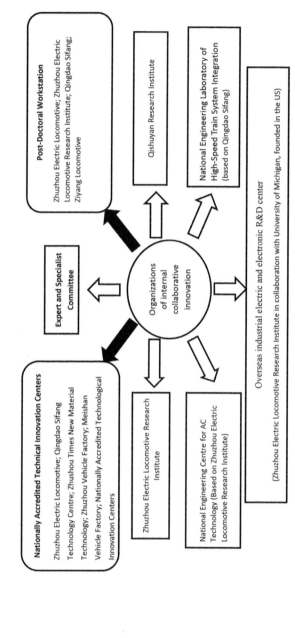

Figure 5.4   Organization of the CSR's internal innovation ecosystem for the high-speed EMU project

To take full advantage of its subsidiary companies, the CSR made a reasonable work distribution, provided relevant support and coordinated R&D and manufacturing capabilities to speed up the innovation process. Take three subsidiary companies – Sifang, Zhuzhou, and Qishuyan – as an example. Sifang (CSR Qingdao Sifang) focused on the technologies of system integration, vehicle body and bogie, and carried out the final assembly. Zhuzhou (Zhuzhou Electric Locomotive Research Institute) undertook the development and manufacture of the network control system and the traction power transmission, including the converter technology and electric traction, the vehicle information control technology, the traction motor technology and the transformer technology. Qishuyan (CSR Qishuyan Research Institute) focused on the technologies on hooking device, basic brake unit, and gear transmission. In addition, CSR Nanjing Puzhen Co., Ltd developed the braking system, as shown in Figure 5.5. Sifang proposed the technical performance requirements, the installation interface, and the working environment of the subsystems according to the whole-vehicle configuration. Zhuzhou and Qishuyan developed the corresponding components and parts, and organized the divergent tests. The vehicle performance verification and acceptance check were also organized by Sifang.

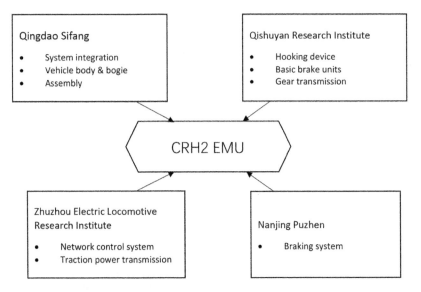

Figure 5.5   Work allocation of the CSR's internal innovation ecosystem for the high-speed EMU project

The External Innovation Ecosystem

In addition to the internal innovation ecosystem, CSR Group orchestrated an innovation ecosystem with vertical and horizontal partners. In terms of vertical partners, the CSR co-created values with upstream suppliers and downstream users. Horizontally, it collaborated closely with the government, research institutes and universities, and even competitors in the same industry. This helped the CSR to gather first-class research and manufacture resources domestically, and build synergies in R&D, design, and testing. The entire project of high-speed EMUs involved 25 top universities in China; 11 domestic leading research institutes; 51 national laboratories and engineering research centers; more than 500 supporting enterprises involving more than 200 experts, specialists and technical leaders; and more than 10 000 engineers and technicians.

Horizontal Alliance

On May 29, 2012, based on the high-speed train action plan jointly signed by the Ministry of Science and Technology and the Ministry of Railways, the CSR initiated the first strategic alliance of high-speed train technological innovation in China, signing 125 cooperation agreements for projects involving 16 organizations, such as Tsinghua University, Zhejiang University, and the Chinese Academy of Sciences (CAS) (Figure 5.6). The alliance was committed to promoting collaborative innovation, as well as enhancing the innovation capability and improving the comprehensive capability of industrialization. In the joint development of the CRH380A, CSR Group and its partner universities also developed talent and exchange-training programs jointly: the universities' talents participated in the design, and the company's talents joined in the research with the university researchers.

Vertical Alliance

CSR Sifang provided technical guidance to the upstream suppliers and downstream customer enterprises; organized collaborative R&D and standard formulation with them; and developed a collaborative innovation alliance with each supplier. It regarded the suppliers' production as a part of the entire corporation's manufacturing system, and required them to participate in the product design and development. Through supervising their production processes, strictly controlling their product quality, and communicating effectively with them to overcome technical difficulties, the collaborative innovation was realized. As a result, the technical level and competitiveness of the entire industrial chain were significantly improved. Table 5.4 summarizes the main stages and actors along the high-speed rail industrial chain.

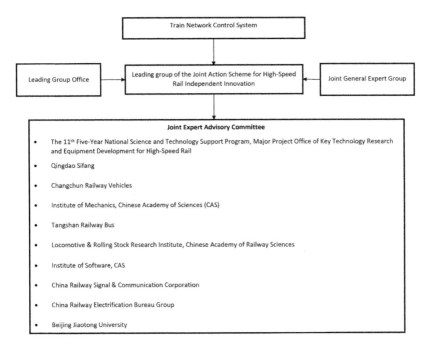

Figure 5.6   The CSR's external innovation ecosystem

The Major Players' Roles in the Ecosystem

In the innovation ecosystem initiated by the CSR, the government formulated strategic planning and major policies and coordinated resource allocation for the major projects; the universities and research institutes focused on research and development and provided advanced technology and research achievements; and the enterprises engaged in applied technology development, process innovation, and relevant commercialization.

The enterprises spotted the technical problems and collected relevant information; guided the direction of technical innovation; and worked with the colleges, universities and research institutes to solve technical problems occurring during the innovation process.

Colleges, universities and research institutes were the main innovators in the high-speed EMU projects. On the one hand, they helped to digest the new technologies imported by the Ministry of Railways and conducted related research on developing technologies that would be more suitable to China's conditions.

Table 5.4   *The industrial chain of high-speed rail*

The high-speed rail industry	Infrastructure and materials	China Railway Group China Railway Construction Corporation China Railway No. 2 Engineering Group Corporation Shanghai Tunnel Engineering Corporation XCMG Construction Machinery ⋮
	Vehicle manufacturer	China South Railway Corporation China North Railway Corporation Northern International Group ⋮
	Accessories and parts	Jinxi Axle Company Xiangtan Electric Manufacturing Corporation AVIC Heavy Machinery Corporation South Huitong Corporation Wolong Electric Group ⋮

Railway communication and monitoring	Huadong Automation Corporation Shenyang Machine Tool Corporation Hefei Sunwin Intelligence Corporation HeNan Splendor Science & Technology Corporation Gem-Year Industrial Corporation ⋮
Operation and logistics	Guangshen Railway Corporation Tianjin Good Hand Railway Holding Co., Ltd China Railway Tielong Container Logistics Co., Ltd Shanghai Shengtong Metro Co., Ltd CMST Development Co., Ltd

On the other hand, they performed frontier exploration of advanced technology for future application.

The Ministry of Railways, which was the central government's institution in the high-speed train ecosystem, organized and implemented the import of high-speed railway technology. It proposed four basic rules: the imported technology must be advanced, mature, applicable, and stable. The Ministry also promoted and accelerated the independent technological innovation of China's high-speed rail. Since the 1990s, the Ministry of Railways had been conducting a large number of technological projects every year, and had worked out a joint action plan with the Ministry of Science and Technology, engaging in importing high-speed railway technologies, enhancing technology accumulation, and mobilizing advantageous research resources nationwide.

For the government, the development and independent innovation of technologies for high-speed EMUs not only promoted the structural and technological upgrade of China's manufacturing industry, but also produced a strong positive effect on a range of industries, including metallurgy, machinery, construction, materials, rubber, electricity, information, precision instruments, and environmental protection. Thus, a large number of star enterprises won international status, and many new products with independent intellectual property rights have been exported, gaining competitive advantages in the international market.

5.6   COORDINATION, INTEGRATION, LEARNING, AND CONTROL IN THE ECOSYSTEM

For rapid technological development and significant innovation, the CSR had, on the one hand, been improving its three-tier supply chain system, including mainframe manufacturer, core equipment manufacturer, and supplement manufacturer. On the other hand, it adopted a "T" framework for collaborative innovation: vertically, it coordinated the partners to devote effort to the two key technologies: traction drive and network control; horizontally, it coordinated the collaborations along the industrial chain.

The Role of Zhuzhou Institute (Zhuzhou Electric Locomotive Research Institute)

To develop the two key technologies of traction drive and network control, Zhuzhou Institute invested more than 3 billion RMB in R&D. Through this effort, Zhuzhou successfully solved the problems related to the CSR's EMUs and extended itself into the two ends of the industrial chain: the upstream of insulated gate bipolar transistors (IGBT) application technology, and the downstream of divergent applications. Based on this strategy, the collaborative innovation drove the entire industrial chain's upgrade, including key materials, processes, core components, large systems, and accessories. For instance, the CRH 1 (eight-axle 9600 kilowatt electric locomotive) promoted localization of the main parts, such as the traction motor fan, traction motor, transformer, high-voltage isolator, earthing switch, and safety interlock box. It also led to the localization of related components in peripheral industries. For example, Zhuzhou Riwang Co., Ltd was a small private factory for processing parts. Collaborating with the Zhuzhou Institute, the company began to supply the converter cabinet for the high-speed train in 2005, and its sales revenue increased by more than 20 times. Therefore, the "T" strategy greatly promoted both the technological development and the economic prosperity of the players along the industrial chain.

Integration of the Three Collaborative Innovation Platforms

To strengthen the foundation of independent innovation, the CSR established three technical platforms for design, manufacture, and product. Based on the high-level technical standards for the three platforms, the CSR developed indexes to regularly evaluate the contents, standards, and effects of the three platforms' development, encouraging its subsidiaries to continuously upgrade their corresponding technical levels of design, manufacture, and product.

The design platform involved design standards, design flow, design method, and product testing. The computer-aided design and manufacturing (CAD/CAM)-integrated operation, the product data management system (PDMS), and the collaboration platform were fully adopted. International advanced design and analysis software, such as PRO/E and ANSYS, were deployed to build the first-class three-dimensional (3D) digital design and verification platform.

The manufacture platform included process research, design, specifications, execution, logistics management, site management, quality control, and equipment manufacturing. On the one hand, the CSR used foreign knowledge to analyze and improve its manufacturing processes. On the other hand, it gradually upgraded the entire platform and developed a solid foundation for the manufacture system. The CSR invested 1 billion RMB in upgrading technologies and constructing manufacturing bases, and achieved the highest production capacity of electric locomotives and EMUs worldwide.

The product platform included the localized, standardized, serialized, modularized vehicles and parts, as well as the relevant technology, performance, quality, reliability, and service. Based on the digestion and absorption of the imported technology, the CSR started the "2211" project to meet the requirements of product serialization, standardization and systematization. "2211" means 2 "high" (high-speed and highland/plateau), 2 "fast" (fast passenger transport and fast cargo transport), 1 "heavy" (heavy loaded cargo transport), and 1 "light" (light rail vehicle). After several years of development, the CSR accomplished a comparatively complete product system of rail transit vehicle. Product performance, quality, and reliability, as well as other important indicators, were in line with international industrial standards.

Through the above measures, the CSR gradually gathered its human, material, and financial resources into the three collaborative innovation platforms (design, manufacture, and product), and its independent innovation capability was steadily strengthened.

The Learning Mechanism

The essence of arranging innovation at the ecosystem level is the mutual transfer and learning of explicit and implicit knowledge among actors such as enterprises, universities, and research institutes. To fully absorb foreign advanced manufacturing technologies, it was necessary to import the complete innovation process and comprehend the foreign technologies during localization. To avoid misinterpretation during the process of absorbing the imported technologies, CSR Sifang developed guidelines for the project of EMUs with a running speed of 200 km/h: "first rigidify, then optimize, and then solidify." Through a range of development and certification activities for the first domestic production of EMUs, the engineers gradually came to a consensus: only by implementing the foreign process and quality control rigidly at first could the local product match the original product's quality.

Furthermore, analyses of imported technical data, physical learning, expert training, technical drawings transformation, technical review, personal explanation, product verification, and summarization were required to comprehensively grasp the key technologies and standard systems. With a complete understanding of the overall technical performance, parameters, structure, main system, and accessory performance of the imported products, the CSR created a technical document system for imported technology that would ensure the standardization and completeness of the imported knowledge.

In the process of digesting and absorbing the imported technology, the front-line staff's work capacity and their understanding of the imported technology played an important role. Therefore, the CSR organized a range of activities for a large number of its core staff, such as class study, observation, and exercise, field training in the foreign factories, and direct discussion with foreign employees. Through these activities, the CSR's employees could witness and appreciate the rigorous and meticulous work style of their foreign peers and learn their advanced work methods. As a result, the CSR and its employees gradually integrated advanced work ideals and methods into the CSR's daily operations, facilitating the digestion and absorption of the imported technologies.

Reducing Risks Through Process Redesign and Quality Management

It is evident that the CSR was coordinating a huge system of collaborative innovation, with all the collaborative risks. Thus, it adopted the following measures to reduce the risks in the process of collaborative innovation and the technical risks resulting from the "railway-speed increase."

First, plan ahead and implement the project step-by-step. In the case of CRH380A, the existing problems with EMUs had been systematically sorted out, and appropriate countermeasures were proposed in the planning stage. In the early stage, it took two years of systematically analyzing the plans and the test results before the CSR could deliver a concrete development scheme. Then, the entire scheme was implemented step-by-step, from the test vehicle CRH2C-Stage I to CRH2C-Stage II with the new front. After comprehensive tests of the vehicle body, traction, bogie, brake, and other major components, the CSR launched the final CRH380A plan.

Second, redesign the entire process, and strictly implement it in the R&D. The CSR strictly followed the four stages of product development: conceptual design, technical design, construction design, and test verification. The CSR conducted sufficient tests and verifications before product delivery and organized tracking tests to be implemented after the delivery. After the new EMUs started to operate, a range of tracking tests were conducted to find and solve possible problems in advance.

Third, quality control. Furthermore, the CSR strictly implemented the policy of "meeting customer needs with quality standards and management," and constantly improved the quality assurance system for long-term quality management and control. In 1997, the CSR passed the ISO9001 standard system certification. In 2008, the reliability-centered quality system was imported. Later, in 2010, CSR Group completed accreditation of the International Railway Industry Standard (IRIS). Based on the principles of systematic analysis and overall planning, as well as step-by-step implementation, the CSR established a complete process control system, including product development, process, procurement, inspection, manufacture, delivery, and after-sales service. Each stage required a complete test process. Moreover, the whole process of quality supervision and management was extended to different manufacturers among the upstream and downstream partners of the industrial chain. All of the above measures enabled the CSR to improve product quality steadily and to achieve the lowest possible product failure rate.

5.7   THE CSR'S SUCCESS AS A STATE-LED INNOVATION ECOSYSTEM

Through continuous R&D, CSR Group not only mastered the core technology of high-speed rail, but also solved various technical problems along the industrial chain; formed its own technical standards; and gradually established a sound position in the international market. From 2010 to 2015, the proportion of high-speed railway's passenger volume to the overall railway system in China increased dramatically, from 8.0 percent to 37.9 percent. By the end of 2016, China's high-speed train system had transported 1.5 billion passengers. According to the Medium- and Long-Term Railway Network Plan issued by the State Development and Reform Commission, the Ministry of Transport, and the China Railway Corporation, by 2025, high-speed rail's mileage would increase to 38 000 km, twice that in 2015. Although the CSR merged with the NSR group in 2015, its great achievements contributed significantly to the subsequent success of Chinese high-speed rail technology. The CSR's innovation experience serves as a model for the way in which a state-led innovation ecosystem manages technological breakthroughs based on mega-projects in the infrastructure sector.

Value Creation for All Parties

The CSR fully utilized the advantages of large state-owned enterprises and successfully orchestrated a mega-project that benefits various innovation actors.

First, due to the development of new technologies and the growing environmental awareness, governments worldwide were increasingly favoring rail transport. There was a strong demand in both domestic and international rail transit equipment markets. Given the giant territory as well as increasing demands for railway transportation, it was important for China to make use of new technologies and take the opportunity to build a high-speed rail system, not only to satisfy market demands, but also to implement the strategies of national rail transit equipment industry and, from a broader perspective, to facilitate a possible leap forward in social and economic development.

Second, the CSR promoted the development of the railway industrial chains through the "T" framework and the government-led collaborative innovation model. Alliances with upstream and downstream enterprises for R&D collaboration and joint development of the technical standards were formed under the CSR's and governmental institutions' leadership. Not only was the company's own competitiveness greatly improved, but the technological and operational levels of the entire industry chain were also improved. CSR Group mastered the nine key technologies of the high-speed train system, and the localization rate of imported technology for the whole vehicle exceeded 75 percent, facilitating the rapid development of China's railway equipment manufacturing industry.

Third, high-speed rail development has also created great economic and social benefits. It has played an important role in accelerating the transformation of China's economic development mode, in promoting the optimization and upgrade of the industrial structure, and in accelerating urbanization. The following are specific ways in which high-speed rail has benefited China. First, the annual passenger volume of the high-speed railway in China has been four to five times more than that of the ordinary railways. It has greatly expanded passenger transport capacity of the entire rail transport system and shortened passengers' travel time. Second, operation of the high-speed rail has facilitated the separation between passenger and cargo transportation. The freight capacity of railway has increased, while the cost of logistics has decreased. Third, the rapid development of the high-speed rail industry and independent innovation capabilities has spawned a number of high-tech innovative enterprises; the high-speed rail industry has developed into a strategic emerging industry with great scale and potential, and has formed complete R&D and manufacturing clusters in many areas. Fourth, as China's high-speed rail construction has adopted a large number of viaducts, the newly built high-speed railways have saved more than 230 000 acres of land and created significant environmental benefits. Fifth, the high-speed rail industry has also provided strong support for stimulating domestic demand and accelerating urbanization. For example, the number of passengers traveling from Beijing to Tianjin increased by 30 percent after the opening of the high-speed intercity line, which greatly promoted efficiency and resource allocation along the line, and balanced urban and rural development.

State-Led Innovation

The government, mainly the Ministry of Railways, was one of the main users of high-speed railway equipment. Therefore, compared to other industries, the innovation ecosystem of high-speed rail projects had strong governmental participation, and the outstanding achievements of China's high-speed rail development are inseparable from national-level policy and the significant investments by relevant government departments (Figure 5.7). The Ministry of Railways integrated the national railway market as the negotiating leverage of technology imports. For such a large market, the international players with the most advanced railway switch technology, ballast-free track technology, and high-speed train technology flocked to the Chinese market. Diversified negotiation effectively avoided price hikes and also ensured the importation of the most advanced technologies. Among all the projects of the Ministry of Railways and other government departments, developing the high-speed rail technology was always prioritized. The total government investment in high-speed train development exceeded 300 million RMB, which ensured sufficient financial support for pertinent technological innovation. In addition, the Ministry of Railways invested 5 percent of its high-speed rail service annual income for further industrial services and technological innovation, providing adequate financial support for the development in key areas such as braking systems, traction systems, and ballastless track fasteners of high-speed EMUs. The government also played a powerful role in integrating resources and coordinating corporations. In short, the import, digestion, absorption, and re-innovation of China's high-speed rail technology could not have been realized without the government-driven, key enterprise-led innovation ecosystem.

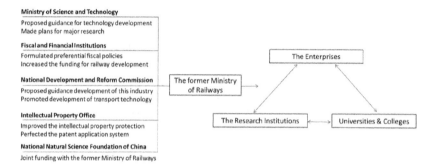

Figure 5.7   The extensive participants of the high-speed rail project

Open Innovation

During the technology-import stage, the CSR adhered to the goal of fully grasping the internationally advanced technologies for high-speed EMUs and high-powered locomotives. Toward this goal, the CSR imported system integration technology and manufacturing technology to promote the import and assimilation of other related technologies. Many of the CSR's companies and R&D institutions adopted a high-level standard for the large-scale technology import to ensure that the imported technology could be used to satisfy the specific needs of Chinese railway transport and could also meet the long-term development goals of the Chinese rail transit equipment industry. For example, the comparatively mature technology of EMUs, supporting a running speed of 200 km/h, was required to be adjusted to support a running speed of 300 km/h. Furthermore, the CSR also developed a localization rate index to evaluate the efficacy of technology absorption. For example, with regard to the imported technology of Kawasaki EMUs with a running speed of 200 km/h, in accordance with the contract, except for first three EMUs imported directly from Japan, all the others were to be manufactured by the CSR. And the localization rate of the deliverable EMUs was required to be 30 percent in the first stage, 50 percent in the second, and 70 percent in the third.

The CSR digested and absorbed the imported knowledge and technologies through collaboration and effective communication between the various enterprises of the industrial chains, as well as through cultivation of talents and teams. Thus, in this first stage, the enterprises' overall technical capabilities were greatly strengthened. Moreover, the significant investment that the CSR made in assimilating the imported technologies accelerated the process of digesting and absorbing the technologies.

In the re-innovation stage, the CSR cultivated the partner enterprises' independent innovation capabilities with the three collaborative innovation platforms: design, manufacture, and product. Furthermore, along with them, the CSR integrated internal and external resources and completed the re-innovation of the imported technologies. For internal collaborative innovation – based on the nationally accredited technology centers, the postdoctoral workstations, and the test and verification centers – pertinent research was conducted on the important and complex issues surrounding the process of importing and assimilating technology. For external collaborative innovation, the CSR gave universities and research institutes free rein to conduct basic research for the re-innovation of the imported technologies, leading to the achievement of world-class technologies within quite a short period and to the CSR's transformation from a manufacturer to an innovator.

5.8   FINAL WORDS REGARDING THE STATE-LED INNOVATION ECOSYSTEM

In the early stage of high-speed train development, the Ministry of Railways was the operator of domestic passenger and cargo transport, as well as the initiator that strongly encouraged the development the high-speed rail with corresponding industrial policies and divergent supportive measures. The success of the high-speed railway project could not have been achieved without the Ministry of Railways acting as the initiator and coordinator. In 2013, the Ministry of Railways was dissolved, and a new large SOE called China Railway General Corporation was established. In 2019, this SOE was renamed the China State Railway Group.

The key features of a state-led innovation ecosystem can be summarized as follows. First, the high-speed train project, a long-term project that entailed a huge and continuous investment, would not have been viable without the strong support of the state banking system. Moreover, as the project covered infrastructure reconstruction across many provinces in China, central government's coordination was indispensable.

Second, the success of this complex product innovation was in line with the open innovation mode and involved rich collaboration and knowledge sharing among various enterprises, universities, and research institutes. Many multinationals also transferred their leading technology to the partners in China; these included Bombardier of Canada for CRH1, Kawasaki of Japan for CRH2, and Siemens of Germany for CRH3.

Third, the Ministry of Railways had the role of institutional end-user to organize intellectuals developing technical standard systems, mobilize resources facilitating the CSR's innovations, and diffuse the developed technology and the system across China.

So far, the cases shared in this book have something in common: the radical innovation projects of the CSR, China Mobile, and State Grid were all directly led or facilitated by the central government. However, readers may wonder: without the advantageous resources and strong support from the central government, how can an SOE actualize remarkable innovations? In fact, there exists such a case, and we will share it in the next chapter.

REFERENCES

Liu, X., Cheng, P., and Chen, A. (2011). Basic research and catch-up in China's high-speed rail industry. *Journal of Chinese Economic and Business Studies*, *9*(4), 349–367.

MOST (2015). Indigenous and integrated innovation driving the boom in China's high-speed rail technologies. *Engineering*, *1*(1), 9–10.

6. The CGN and engineering innovation in nuclear power construction

6.1 INTRODUCTION

China's central government has identified several strategic emerging industries that are vital for the country's technological, economic, and social development. The government will therefore take measures to support the strategic areas, including energy conservation and environmental protection, the emerging information technologies, biological technologies, new energy and new energy vehicles, high-end equipment manufacturing, and new materials. As an important component of the new energy industry, nuclear power has been developed with enormous support from the central government. At present, 57 nuclear reactors are operating or under construction, and additional reactors are being planned across the country. It is estimated that China will have 100 nuclear reactors by 2030.

In the 1980s, the power shortage in the Yangtze River Delta and Pearl River Delta could not be solved by simply transmitting power from other areas because of the technological limitations on power transmission. Thus, the nuclear power program was initiated, and Qinshan Phase I Project and Daya Bay Project were launched in 1985 and 1987. After a long period of stagnation, fast progress finally took hold in 2005. Following the principle of "combining foreign technology transfers with domestic design and production," the domestically optimized technology for the second generation of pressurized water reactors (PWRs), which had been under debate for years, was finally approved as the foundation for further technological development (Zhou and Zhang, 2010).

As China entered the 21st century, air pollution and coal shortage had become critical concerns for the sustainable development of China, while nuclear energy was deemed a favorable option for supplying power in the future. According to the Eleventh Five-Year Plan (2006–2010), nuclear power would be the appropriate power source, and the Medium- and Long-Term Nuclear Power Development Plan (2005–2020) stated that China's nuclear power generation capacity was to be increased to 40 GWh by 2020. With a number of supportive policies, by the end of 2005, four types of self-designed reactors based on Generation II technology had been put into use (CNP300, CNP600, CNP1000, and CPR1000). As of September 2010, 19 of the 25 generator sets under construction had been designed by Chinese engineers (Chen et al., 2016; Zhou et al., 2011).

The Fukushima nuclear accident in 2011 caused the termination or suspension of the operation and construction of nuclear power plants in European countries such as Germany, Italy, and Switzerland (Mu et al., 2015). Based on improving the evaluation and approval process of new projects, the Chinese government put great effort into enhancing the safety standards in order to further promote nuclear power's development. Furthermore, according to the Twelfth Five-Year Plan (2011–2015), the third-generation nuclear power plants were explicitly encouraged (Wang and Chen, 2012), which in turn implied new opportunities and challenges. Currently, the technologies of the new reactors being built in China vary from Generation II (CPR600, CPR1000, CNP1000 and AES91) and Generation III (AP1000 and ERP) to Generation IV (HTR-PM) (Wang and Chen, 2012).

The data in this chapter come mainly from interviews we conducted from May 20–22, 2014, when we visited the China General Nuclear Power Group (CGN) for intensive interaction and observation. We also collected considerable secondary data from the CGN's internal and published reports. With the support of the China Enterprise Confederation, we conducted multiple interviews with 18 experts holding a variety of positions within the CGN ecosystem, who were from research and development (R&D) departments, equipment manufacturers, constructors, and suppliers. Most of them had been associated with this industry for over ten years. The interviews were semi-structured and combined with observations, and each lasted around 1.5 hours on average. We conducted interviews in the general manager's office on the CGN's strategy and reform process; in the project management department on project management, supply chain management, and collaboration; in the engineering and R&D department on R&D management; and in the human resource department on organizational management. Additional insightful information was acquired through the interview with the general manager, Guogang Shu, on May 22, 2014.

6.2   CHINA GENERAL NUCLEAR POWER GROUP

Along with China's policy of reform and opening up, as well as the government's resolution to promote nuclear power, China General Nuclear Power Group (CGN, formerly known as China Guangdong Nuclear Power Group) was founded in September 1994. Although it was a locally managed state-owned enterprise (SOE), with its achievements and the strategic implications, the CGN is currently under the direct supervision of the State-owned

Assets Supervision and Administration Commission (of the State Council) of China. As a giant in clean energy production, it has 34 subsidiaries.

Since its inception, the CGN has made an unrelenting effort to fulfill its mission of "developing clean energy to benefit mankind" and to realize its vision of "building one of the world's top clean energy enterprises." By the end of May 2014, the installed capacity of the CGN's operating nuclear generating units had reached 11.62 million kWh, and the capacity of new 13 units under construction would achieve 15.5 million kWh. In addition, the CGN owns an installed capacity of 5.0 million kWh of wind power and a total capacity of 0.5 million kWh of solar photovoltaic power. From 2007 to 2014, the CGN's R&D spending increased (see Figure 6.1), and seven state-level nuclear power R&D centers were established (Chen et al., 2016), leading to its making great strides in distributed energy, nuclear technology application, and energy conservation technologies. With the trend of SOEs' outbound expansion starting around 2004, the CGN also developed its businesses and operations in the United Kingdom (UK), Romania, and South Africa. The CGN's overseas activities included establishing specialized and compatible infrastructures for power plant construction and operation, fuel supply, as well as research and development. By the end of 2014, its annual sales had increased by 18.8 percent to 19.33 billion CNY, and its annual profit increased by 35.6 percent to 6.88 billion CNY (Chen et al., 2016).

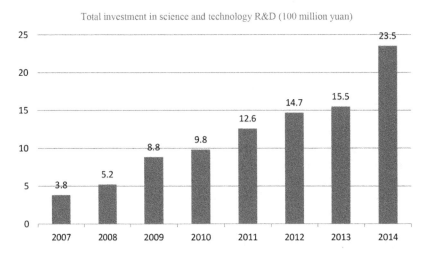

Figure 6.1   Annual R&D expenditures of the CGN (2007–2014)

6.3   EVOLUTION OF THE CGN'S INNOVATION ECOSYSTEM

Development Stages

From the perspective of the innovation ecosystem, the CGN's innovation in the nuclear power construction projects progressed through three stages: incubation, figuration, and self-renewal. The three stages overlapped and boosted each other in a loop (Moore, 1993).

After the completion of the Daya Bay plant, which had relied entirely on imported foreign technologies, the CGN geared up its technological improvements and innovation by investing over US$15 million yearly, starting in 1994 (Chen et al., 2016). Based on its experience and collaboration with domestic companies, the CGN's design and engineering capabilities were greatly improved. In 1997, the construction of the Lingao Nuclear Power Station I (LNPS I) was launched. With the CGN's quality and responsibility system, a strand of independent innovation initiatives – including engineering management, construction and installation, debugging and production preparation, and parts of design and equipment localization – were carried out. During the LNPS I project, the CGN adopted 52 important technological improvements that met the leading international standards. Meanwhile, the CGN developed good relations with many domestic construction and installation companies through collaborative design and engineering, as well as through its purchase of a whole set of equipment from them. Accumulating valuable experience in power plant construction, equipment installation, project management, as well as testing and operation, a number of companies within the ecosystem gained specialized technological knowledge and capabilities, and the average localization rate of the equipment and engineering reached 30 percent (Chen et al., 2016). Furthermore, other institutions, such as energy companies, financial companies and provincial governments, started to engage in the nuclear reactor projects and became indispensable components of the nuclear power ecosystem. Table 6.1 briefly illustrates the three stages of the innovation ecosystem and the associated challenges.

Table 6.2 gives an overview of the mass nuclear power construction projects led by CGN Group.

Stage I: Incubation (1987–2004)

With imported technologies from France, the CGN began to work on the Guangdong Daya Bay Nuclear Power Station (GNPS), which was the first large commercial nuclear power station in mainland China. Back then, the

Table 6.1   *Challenges in different stages of the innovation ecosystem*

Stages	Challenges
Ecosystem incubation	Collaboration among subsidiaries and continuous growth. Filling missing links of the value chains, and initiating a process of rapid ongoing improvement.
Ecosystem figuration	Broader collaboration along the value chains and expansion to relevant new domains. Significant growth and profitability of the subsidiaries, as well as reasonably stable value-adding components and processes of the ecosystem. Participation of suppliers and customers, and their sustained dependence on the ecosystem.
Ecosystem self-renewal	Prosperity of the entire ecosystem. Cooperation with rival ecosystems and other stakeholders, as well as balance among stability, change, and new innovations in new environments.

Table 6.2   *Nuclear power projects under operation, construction, or preparation in China by the CGN*

Owner	Name of nuclear power project	Gross power (million kWh)	Total (million kWh)	Reactor type
CGN	Daya Bay	2 × 984	6.11	PWR(M310)
	Lingao I	2 × 990		PWR(M310)
	Lingao II	2 × 1080		PWR(CPR1000)
	Hongyanhe	4 × 1080	29.76	CPR1000
	Ningde	4 × 1080		CPR1000
	Yangjiang	(3 + 3) × 1080		CPR1000
	Taishan	2 × 1750		EPR
	Fangchanggang(Hongsha)	2 × 1080		CPR1000
	Lufeng	6 × 1080		CPR1000
	Xianning(Dafan)	2 × 1250		AP1000

industrial chain of commercial nuclear power was quite incomplete and uncompetitive. The CGN acted as the coordinator of the engineering project by conducting the procurement and assisting in the design and construction. The core parts were exclusively constructed by the French engineers, and they controlled the crucial technologies. To illustrate the exclusive control exerted by the French, even the stones used to protect the plant from tide waves were imported from France.

Driven by the government's resolution on developing nuclear power, as a locally managed SOE at that time, the CGN took the initiative to facilitate indigenous and domestic technological development by encouraging collaboration between its subsidiaries and creating a stable interdependence between them. Another important measure that the CGN took was the establishment of a reliable quality control and responsibility system, which enabled continuous and efficient improvements of the final products' performance and quality. Through these measures, the CGN integrated resources across its subsidiaries and established collaborations with external business partners. In these ways, the CGN initiated a series of massive innovation projects and facilitated establishment of the innovation ecosystem. Figure 6.2 illustrates the ecosystem structure at stage I.

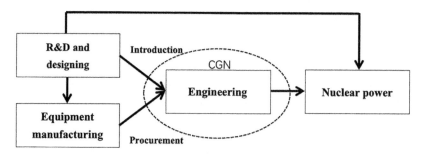

Figure 6.2   Ecosystem structure at stage I

Stage II: Figuration (2005–2010)

In this stage, rapidly expanding construction and manufacturing contributed significantly to the power plant development, and the CGN comprehensively mastered the second generation of nuclear technology. Furthermore, deploying more than 50 technological improvements (Chen et al., 2016), the CGN began construction of the Lingao Nuclear Power Station II (LNPS II) in 2005; for this project, the localization rate of equipment and components increased from LNPS I's 30 percent to 64 percent. The core technology of the pressurized water reactor at million-kilowatt grade, as well as the improved pressurized water reactor (CPR1000), were developed during the LNPS II project. More power stations based on the CPR1000 reactor were built, such as Hongyanhe in Liaoning Province (HNP), Ningde in Fujian Province (NNP), and Yangjiang in Guangdong Province (YNP).

With the rapid shift to the third-generation technology, such as AP1000 and EPR, the competition between the various technical routes became increasingly fierce. In the Chinese market, several international giants were attracted and competing intensively with each other. This created more challenges for the CGN, and enhancing collaborations along the value chain could be the effective way to increase the CGN's market share. To achieve this goal, the CGN adopted the model of architectural engineering (AE) to eliminate the barriers between its organizational departments and the regions in which its businesses were conducted. This could also mitigate the problems of segmentation and dispersal of strengths in power plant design and construction among multiple similar projects. The AE model had emerged in the United States (US) in the 1960s and 1970s, offering a complete set of solutions for engineering management and an integration of design and construction. For the CGN, providing systemic and integrated services for building nuclear power stations – such as design, engineering, and construction management – involved different equipment manufacturers and power generation enterprises. Based on these integrated services, the CGN achieved effective control over safety, quality, and scheduling in large-scale and complex engineering projects. As research institutes or engineering enterprises working alone cannot ensure the success of a project, the CGN further encouraged all the companies of the value chain to serve the potential market through stimulating their initiatives and their responsibilities for meeting the final users' demands. Collaborations along the value chain were also formed, and the win–win synergy started to emerge. For example, one of the CGN's suppliers – the Dongfang Electric Corporation (DEC) – suffered greatly due to the overdue issue of its tube manufacturing. As an ecosystem leader, the CGN proactively cooperated with the DEC to solve the problems with detailed records of the source-tracking process. This significantly shortened the manufacture period of quality tubes and established interdependence as well as trust for sustainable collaboration between the CGN and its suppliers.

In the ecosystem figuration stage, players within the ecosystem saw rapid growth and high profitability. Thus, a robust community was formed through creating shared values along the value chain and collective technological improvement. More importantly, the returns increased with a snowball effect, and it became increasingly difficult for the ecosystem players to switch to other ecosystems since the opportunity costs could be rather high. The interdependency and constant collaborative innovation therefore played a critical role in maintaining the ecosystem and improving its overall performance. Figure 6.3 depicts the CGN's innovation ecosystem structure at the figuration stage.

Stage III: Self-renewal (2011–2014)

Similar to the threat of environmental change to a natural ecosystem, an innovation ecosystem may waver, and even shatter, due to the rise of new technological paradigms or sudden changes in institutional environments, including governmental regulations and macroeconomic situations. Ever since the severe earthquake and tsunami that caused profound damage to the Fukushima nuclear power plant in Japan in 2011, there have been increasing concerns about the safety of nuclear power plants, as well as outspoken opposition to

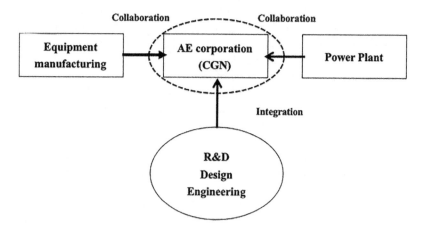

Figure 6.3   Ecosystem structure at stage II

nuclear power in the US and Europe. The response has been more stringent quality and safety standards to reduce the potential risks and threats to people and the environment.

The CGN, in particular, responded to these circumstances by extending the value chains of the existing ecosystem to create better collaborative innovation and, as a result, achieve a higher level of safety and quality. With a number of subsequent reforms, the CGN became an influential ecosystem coordinator, with more players, more extensive collaborations, and more synergies. As shown in Figure 6.4, A1 represents the position of the CGN in the Chinese nuclear power industry. It was surrounded by numerous large and medium-sized enterprises (B1, B2, ..., Bn) providing key parts and complete equipment to the CGN; these firms operate under the CGN's supervision and strict standards. These large and medium-sized enterprises were also surrounded by a larger number of small-sized enterprises (C1, C2, ..., Cn), supplying key auxiliary products and technology to them. Although these smaller (C-level) firms were directly associated with the large and medium-sized enterprises (B-level), they still needed to meet the standards developed by the CGN. Further, additional relevant players were involved in the network-structured ecosystem, such as financial agencies, R&D institutions, and universities (D1, D2, ..., Dn). All of these enterprises constituted an ecosphere based on mutual learning and collaboration with the CGN.

For more potential resources and technical support to develop better and safer technologies, the CGN collaborated with similar innovation ecosystems whose central players are rivals of the CGN, such as the China National Nuclear

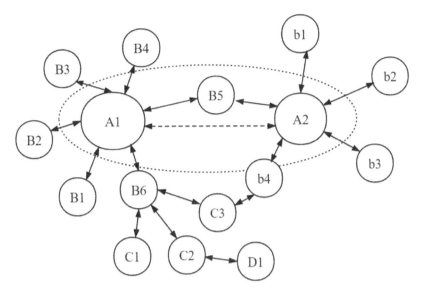

Figure 6.4   Ecosystem structure at stage III

Corporation (CNNC) and the State Power Investment Corporation (SPIC) (A2). With this auspicious ecosystem, based on the prevalent Generation III technologies (AP1000 and ERP), the CGN accomplished significant progress in further innovation with its own intellectual rights (for example, ACPR1000+). Moreover, collaborating with its competitor the CNNC, the CGN accomplished one of the most advanced Generation III technologies, HPR1000, which amazed the world. From another perspective, the CGN's ecosystem facilitated significant technology spillover: the developed generic technologies and equipment were also well-suited to relevant and adjacent industries, whose technological foundations were also strengthened along with the development of the CGN's innovation ecosystem.

Nevertheless, when a firm, especially a technology-based firm, starts to expand its business from a single successful bid or project to numerous similar projects, it faces growing complexities, and its complex product system (CoPS) involves collaborations with other partner firms (Frels et al., 2003; Leonard-Barton, 1992; Porter, 2008; Prahalad and Hamel, 1990). The ecosystem perspective serves as a powerful tool to look into the process and details of the firm's growth. As discussed above, the interdependency and co-evolution of the actors, based on their mutual producer–user relationship, constituted the foundation and dynamics of the CGN's innovation ecosystem, facilitating its boundary extension and the symbiosis within its boundaries (Iansiti and

Richards, 2006; Kandiah and Gossain, 1998; Thorelli, 1986; Willianson and De Meyer, 2012). Compared to the market system, an ecosystem involves divergent stakeholders but with shared objectives and even identities. As the ecosystem evolves, it is easy to see the enhancement of the core business; however, the more complex evolution of the ecosystem's technologies, value networks, and dynamic capabilities plays a more profound role in its prosperity.

Technological Evolution

Different from the technological development of a single firm, the evolution of an ecosystem's technologies relies more on the interdependency among the member companies' technologies and the ecosystem's environmental forces, such as the challenges of developing new technologies and the surging opportunities to apply old technologies. To deal with the interdependencies that are inherent in an innovation ecosystem, various activities are necessary, such as balancing the interplay between focal and complementary technologies; competing for dominant technological designs; and seeking a balance between the companies' accumulated experiences and specific requirements of parallel projects at multiple levels (Chen et al., 2016). All of these challenges and actions require the focal ecosystem facilitator to take the initiative to foster a proper climate for the ecosystem's sustainable development, especially at its early stage. How, then, did the CGN achieve this very complex task of creating a successful innovation ecosystem?

As a state-owned enterprise in a developing country that was dedicated to catching up with developed countries, the CGN deployed the learning-by-doing mode, which significantly drove its technical development. Nuclear power stations, an extremely complex product, are non-decomposable and hardly reproducible. The CGN, therefore, imported French technologies and developed effective communication with its French supplier. By virtue of effective communication and benchmarking, the CGN gradually accumulated relevant knowledge of the advanced technologies with its external and internal learning processes, and it then developed the capability to interpret and manipulate that knowledge for further technological improvements.

To catch up with the third-generation technologies, the CGN imported two European Pressurized Reactor (EPR) units designed by the French company AREVA with nuclear fuel components. The CGN's learning capabilities allowed the Chinese company to develop the necessary know-how. During the localization process, the CGN started to collaborate with local engineering and construction companies. By extending its learning processes and achieving mutual learning, the CGN and its partners accumulated and grasped more comprehensive knowledge. Afterwards, the CGN started to replicate the technological localization and project operation experiences in different regions with specific circumstances. By adopting the AE model, the CGN formulated a user-oriented technology and knowledge management system that integrated design and construction, and the firm's own capabilities evolved from know-what to know-how and to know-why (Desouza, 2005). To improve its overall technological level, the CGN established extensive strategic alliances with component manufacturers and integrators for more comprehensive knowledge exchange and subsequent innovation.

Before becoming a large, worldwide nuclear power equipment manufacturer and a key supplier for the CGN, the Dongfang Electric Corporation's (DEC) first order from the CGN was a steel tube with a diameter of over 1 meter. Originally, the DEC had planned to complete the manufacture within three months, but as the quality could not meet the CGN's requirements, the development took one year to complete. Usually, the manufacturing process of nuclear-grade products in China follows very strict procedures, with all relevant tests completed under the supervision of the purchaser and the National Nuclear Security Administration. The CGN's product quality requirements actually helped the DEC to establish a high-level document management system: detailed records of all procedures and operation processes were well maintained, so that the source of any problems could be traced, from raw materials to finished products. For quality control, the DEC and the CGN jointly developed a delivery mechanism that applied to both the relevant documents and the final projects: only when both the documents and projects were finished could the DEC's final products be accepted. Based on the AE model and collaboration with the CGN, a culture of architectural nuclear safety influenced every aspect of the DEC's production.

Similarly, by instituting co-specialization and co-design with partners such as the DEC (Ceccagnoli and Jiang, 2013; Rong, 2011), the CGN was able to develop its own technologies based on French ones, such as CPR1000 and CPR1000+. Then, to a great extent, the CGN was able to achieve independent design, construction, and operation of nuclear power plants based on CPR1000 and CPR1000+, such as the Guangxi Fangchenggang Phase I plant with a localization rate of 85 percent. For further co-development of innovation capabilities, the CGN developed open interfaces with local research institutions, universities, and even competitors, to exchange complementary resources and technologies. These initiatives greatly facilitated a benign climate of open innovation and further prosperity of the innovation ecosystem. Figure 6.5 depicts the technological evolution of the CGN's innovation ecosystem.

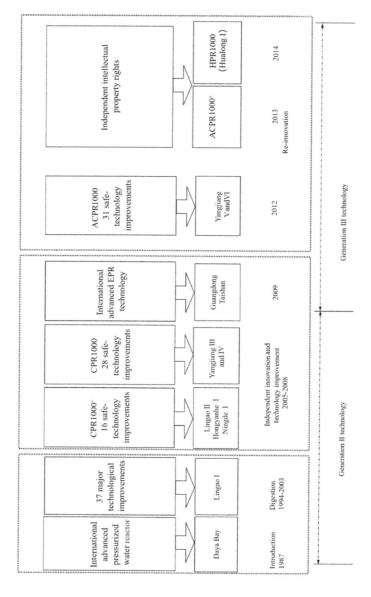

Figure 6.5   Evolution of the technologies

Expanding Value Networks

Technological evolution is the foundation of the innovation ecosystem's development. Yet without continuous value creation and the prosperous expansion of value networks as outcomes, the ecosystem's sustainability could be jeopardized. Schumpeter's theory of innovation underlines the importance of technology and the novel combination of resources, but much effort in practice has been dedicated to building protective barriers to maximize the profits of "innovators," profiting from the intellectual property protection regime and investment in complementary assets. Yet according to the value chain perspective, actors located at every part and stage of a value chain may create value to enlarge the business "pie" (Porter and Kramer, 2011). Indeed, in such an interconnected world, few innovations create value on a stand-alone basis, while most innovations require complementary products, technologies, services, and inputs or components. However, the "value chain" lens has a number of limitations, such as mechanistic linear thinking and partial perspective, and it assumes that value remains "in the product," while ignoring externalities and close cooperative and symbiotic relationships between a company and its customers, suppliers, and other partners (Pierce, 2009).

Comparatively, the perspective of innovation ecosystem suggests that value creation depends not only on products, but also on the interplays between companies. Instead of merely focusing on dyadic interplay, networked interactions, containing both cooperation and competition, and short-term and long-term interplay between the networked enterprises, are highlighted. Value creation between ecosystem partners not only refers to satisfying customers' needs, but also indicates a certain climate and culture that encourages collaborative initiatives, knowledge sharing, and mutual trust. With such benign culture or climate, more diverse collaborative innovation and value co-creation will come into existence, which in turn will extend or create divergent value chains. From a holistic perspective, the entire ecosystem can be viewed as a complex network embedded in various value co-creation relationships, some of which last longer than others. The value networks may expand and evolve as long as the collaboration and competition interplays among the ecosystem companies better satisfy the dynamic change of customers' preferences.

To fulfill the national mission, the CGN started its journey by collaborating with a few suppliers for its core business development. However, to grow the business and increase the task challenges and project complexities, the CGN needed more partners with specialized knowledge and capabilities. Apparently, at the early stage, the CGN's internal management of value creation could not function well with extensive collaborations in place. Deploying the architectural engineering (AE) model, the CGN gradually managed to co-create value for users with partners in an extended network (Peppard and Rylander, 2006).

However, the journey was never smooth. On the one hand, every player in the ecosystem strategically tried to differentiate itself from others in order to obtain more resources and even occupy a central position in the ecosystem. On the other hand, it was quite challenging to develop a value-sharing approach that would be accepted and implemented multilaterally, as it had long been common practice for an individual company to simply maximize its own profits for its final performance assessment. Furthermore, along with the increase in parallel projects, the chance of disputes over resource and asset allocation and information exchange inevitably grew. Obviously, the CGN faced challenges in power control, culture development, and coordination and organization. Unless it dealt with these challenges, value co-creation at the ecosystem level could not be realized, and the value network could not be formed. Eventually, after comprehensive reforms, the CGN maintained its central position in the ecosystem and successfully developed a proper culture and system for collaboration, transparent governance, operations, value sharing, and performance measurement, all of which greatly facilitated the value co-creation among enterprises and the formation of value networks (Ethiraj, 2007; Liu and Rong, 2015).

Along with the evolution of the CGN's innovation ecosystem, the value network expanded, and more stakeholders, such as local governments, universities, and research institutions, joined in. Based on continuous value creation for end-users and the assurance that the business fruits would be shared, the cooperation between ecosystem actors was deepened and broadened. The CGN adjusted its role accordingly and became more engaged in training, evaluating performance, as well as in building industrial parks and security platforms. For instance, Guangdong Taishan Industrial Park, Shenzhen Baolong Industrial Park, and Guangzhou Nansha Industrial Park were established under the CGN's leadership, and these science parks attracted numerous leading domestic and overseas companies. Industrial clusters of nuclear power equipment thus formed, further facilitating the value network's growth at various levels. According to the CGN's general manager, Guogang Shu:

> The difficulty of innovation lies in value and concept. The nature of collaboration is a liability system responsible for the final results. The key point is how to meet all kinds of requirements of the stakeholders and how to make common progress and establish a symbiotic relationship. Therefore, by assisting suppliers to improve their capabilities, the overall level of the nuclear industry in China has achieved a major breakthrough, which in turn provides the CGN a better environment. The CGN has put great efforts in increasing shared interests, but it does not imply a value loss for the CGN.

Upgrading Dynamic Capabilities

An abstract but rather prevalent concept, "dynamic capability" is commonly adopted to discuss a focal firm's survival and competitive advantages in changing environments (Teece, 2007). Indeed, there are several major schools of thought: some view dynamic capability as the ability to integrate internal and external skills and resources of a firm; some take it as a set of routines with which a firm's resources are properly allocated; and some suggest different levels of dynamic capability throughout a firm's development. It is difficult to consider only one of the viewpoints exclusively, since each one has its own significant explanatory power.

To a great extent, strategic orientation is an important driver for a company to develop its dynamic capability. Voss and Voss (2000) suggest that strategic orientation is threefold: customer, competitor, and technology. In such an increasingly competitive and networked world, the "crucial battle" is no longer between individual firms, but "between networks of firms," and strategy is fast becoming "the art of managing assets that one does not own" (Iansiti and Levien, 2004b). Customers' demands are becoming more and more compounded; competitors are evolving to be increasingly versatile; technology is growing increasingly complex and advanced; and more stakeholders, such as suppliers and partners and even the government, have to be involved simultaneously for a company to achieve sustainable development (Autio and Thomas, 2014; Iansiti and Levien, 2004a; Siqueira et al., 2014). Thus, again, the perspective of the ecosystem becomes more valuable since it introduces more comprehensiveness, rather than merely understanding target customers' changing preferences or monitoring competitors' behaviors.

In an ecosystem, being ready to be ahead of your direct rivals may not lead to any advantages if your complementors are not ready. In such a context, a firm may need to upgrade its dynamic capability to slow its development pace and co-explore long-term opportunities with its partners, especially complementors.

While a company that plays the role of orchestrator in an ecosystem can create opportunities, it will also face challenges and risks (Adner, 2006). In addition to maintaining its irreplaceability, an ecosystem orchestrator also needs to formulate "game rules" for the ecosystem. The dynamic capability of an innovation ecosystem constitutes the foundation of its competitive advantage over other innovation ecosystems. To a great extent, the ecosystem's dynamic capability is based on the leading company's dynamic capability in designing and cultivating a suitable climate for other companies to develop their own dynamic capability of co-developing technologies and co-creating values.

Before becoming the leader, the CGN undoubtedly started from zero in developing the dynamic capability of an innovation ecosystem. For a product as complex as nuclear power plants, the CGN had to integrate many resources, components, and technologies at the beginning, as it had almost none back then. Thus, its dynamic capability was reflected mainly in its integration of internal activities and external technologies and activities. While learning from the imported technologies, the CGN formed its organizational procedure management and routines. High-level coherence, repetition, and experimentation enabled the company's tasks to be completed better and faster. Those were critical bases for the CGN's subsequent leading role and co-development with its partners.

When the CGN gradually grasped the key knowledge and skills in design, procurement, and construction, it started to set high-level standards for its partners in order to ensure quality and to facilitate its partners to meet those standards based on its accumulated experience and the co-specialization. However, the prior management structure and routines could not support the increasing co-development and co-specialization. To cope with this, the CGN adopted the AE model, and correspondingly put more effort into organizational and managerial reconfiguration, including decentralization, local autonomy enhancement, and implementation of the marketization mechanism. Meanwhile, the CGN further promoted quality and schedule control among all its partners so that project management was strengthened. It was the capability of reconfiguration that enabled the CGN to support more parallel projects as well as more in-depth collaborations and technology co-development with its partners. This remarkably transformed the CGN's asset structure and role in the ecosystem, while the ecosystem's product and service quality were continuously upgraded based on risk- and cost-sharing among the partners.

In the third stage, the CGN began to help its partners develop their core capabilities. Based on its role and influence, it developed a platform that allowed a large number of enterprises to leverage the CGN's resources to increase their productivity and stability. Furthermore, based on the platform, the CGN founded several joint R&D centers that include most of the top-level nuclear power equipment manufacturers. These R&D centers conducted open and fruitful research to realize the localization of nuclear power equipment, and cultivated a culture of mutual trust among the ecosystem partners. Thus, the CGN and its partners sensed, and even created, more opportunities for collaboration, joint innovations, and business development. With the development of shared communication patterns, as well as reasonably institutionalized collaboration approaches, knowledge could be better shared, and technology co-development could be better realized. The firms gained benefits and, in turn, made investments in leveraging this platform, and began to depend on it for their success. This created a virtuous cycle through which a broad variety of firms co-created values and achieved high levels of productivity, stability, and innovativeness. Eventually, the dynamic capabilities and competences of the enterprises in the ecosystem co-evolved (Liu and Rong, 2015). Figure 6.6 presents the evolution of technology, value networks, and dynamic capabilities of the innovation ecosystem for nuclear power construction in the three stages: incubation, figuration, and self-renewal.

6.4   THE CGN'S SUCCESS IN ENGINEERING INNOVATION

As a latecomer to the international nuclear power industry, the CGN has made remarkable achievements: from possessing little knowledge, to generating abundant and comprehensive knowledge; and from solo development, to co-development, co-design, and co-creation. From 2011 to 2018, the CGN's power generation increased from 40 500 to 157 000 GWh. In 2018, it achieved an operating income of 50.828 billion CNY, with an annual growth of 11.4 percent. Currently, the CGN has more than 50 percent market share in the field of nuclear power generation in China. In addition to the Hinkley Point nuclear power project in the UK, the CGN has signed memoranda or intent agreements for nuclear power cooperation with enterprises or governments in more than 20 countries. In the near future, the CGN will gradually expand market share in Central and Eastern Europe, Southeast Asia, West Asia, and Africa with systemic risk control.

Different from the China National Nuclear Corporation (CNNC) and the State Power Investment Corporation (SPIC), which are centrally managed SOEs, as a locally managed SOE at the time (before it started to be centrally managed by the State-owned Assets Supervision and Administration Commission), the CGN had to find its own way to sustainable development. On the one hand, by selling electric power to Hong Kong, the CGN earned considerable financial support. On the other hand, it put much effort into collaborating with its partners for technological development. Apparently, an innovation ecosystem cannot form and evolve without collaborative efforts, and it thus depends on comprehensive interactions among players and effective management. For centrally managed SOEs such as the CSR and State Grid, discussed in previous chapters, their advantages regarding comprehensive supports from the central government and affiliated research institutions greatly facilitated the formation of their ecosystems. However, for locally managed SOEs such as the CGN, allying with other partners for their complementary resources and capabilities has been essential to the success of massive infrastructure innovation projects. Playing as a leader as well as a coach, the CGN chose to comprehensively restructure itself, focusing on co-developing technologies and co-creating values with partners while upgrading technical

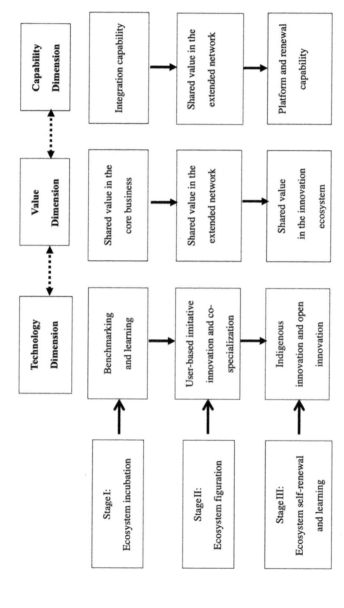

Figure 6.6　　Evolution of technology, value, and capability at the three stages

standards for holistic quality enhancement. Throughout this process, its dynamic capabilities grew substantially; not only for its own development, but also for the ecosystem's development. With great effort, the CGN actualized the synergy among technological innovation, value creation, and dynamic capability development for the innovation ecosystem, and all of its efforts to create a sustainable ecosystem were, in turn, greatly helpful in enhancing the CGN's competence and staying power.

REFERENCES

Adner, R. (2006). Match your innovation strategy to your innovation ecosystem. *Harvard Business Review, 84*(4), 1–11.

Autio, E., and Thomas, L. (2014). Innovation ecosystem: Implications for innovation management. In M. Dodgson, D.M. Gann, and N. Phillips (eds), *The Oxford Handbook of Innovation Management* (pp. 204–288). Oxford: Oxford University Press.

Ceccagnoli, M., and Jiang, L. (2013). The cost of integrating external technologies: Supply and demand drivers of value creation in the markets for technology. *Strategic Management Journal, 34*(4), 404–425.

Chen, J., Liu, X., and Hu, Y. (2016). Establishing a CoPs-based innovation ecosystem to enhance competence – the case of CGN in China. *International Journal of Technology Management, 72*(1/2/3), 144–170.

Desouza, K.C. (2005). *New Frontiers of Knowledge Management.* London: Palgrave Macmillan.

Ethiraj, S.K. (2007). Allocation of inventive effort in complex product systems. *Strategic Management Journal, 28*(6), 563–584.

Frels, J.K., Shervani, T., and Srivastava, R.K. (2003). The integrated networks model: Explaining resource allocations in network markets. *Journal of Marketing, 67*(1), 29–45.

Iansiti, M., and Levien, R. (2004a). Strategy as ecology. *Harvard Business Review, 82*(3), 68–81.

Iansiti, M., and Levien, R. (2004b). *The Keystone Advantage: What the New Dynamics of Business Ecosystems Mean for Strategy, Innovation, and Sustainability.* Boston, MA: Harvard Business Press.

Iansiti, M., and Richards, G.L. (2006). Information technology ecosystem: Structure, health, and performance. *Antitrust Bulletin, 51*(1), 77.

Kandiah, G., and Gossain, S. (1998). Reinventing value: The new business ecosystem. *Strategy and Leadership, 26*(5), 28–33.

Leonard-Barton, D. (1992). Core capabilities and core rigidities: A paradox in managing new product development. *Strategic Management Journal, 13*(2), 111–125.

Liu, G., and Rong, K. (2015). The nature of the co-evolutionary process complex product development in the mobile computing industry's business ecosystem. *Group and Organization Management, 40*(6), 809–842.

Moore, J.F. (1993). Predators and prey: A new ecology of competition. *Harvard Business Review, 71*(3), 75–83.

Mu, R., Zuo, J., and Yuan, X. (2015). China's approach to nuclear safety – from the perspective of policy and institutional system. *Energy Policy, 76*, 161–172.

Peppard, J., and Rylander, A. (2006). From value chain to value network: Insights for mobile operators. *European Management Journal, 24*(2), 128–141.

Pierce, L. (2009). Big losses in ecosystem niches: How core firm decisions drive complementary product shakeouts. *Strategic Management Journal, 30*(3), 323–347.

Porter, M.E. (2008). *Competitive Strategy: Techniques for Analyzing Industries and Competitors*. New York: Simon & Schuster.

Porter, M.E., and Kramer, M.R. (2011). Creating shared value. *Harvard Business Review, 89*(1–2), 62–77.

Prahalad, C.K., and Hamel. G. (1990). The core competence of the corporation. *Harvard Business Review, 68*(3), 79–91.

Rong, K. (2011). Nurturing business ecosystems from firm perspectives: Lifecycle, nurturing process, construct, configuration pattern. Doctoral dissertation, University of Cambridge.

Siqueira, A.C.O., Monzoni, M.P., Mariano, S.R., Moraes, J., Branco, P.D., and Coelho, A.M. (2014). Innovation ecosystems in Brazil: Promoting social entrepreneurship and sustainability. In *Emerging Research Directions in Social Entrepreneurship* (pp. 127–142). Dordrecht: Springer.

Teece, D.J. (2007). Explicating dynamic capabilities: The nature and microfoundations of sustainable enterprise performance. *Strategic Management Journal, 28*(13), 1319–1350.

Thorelli, H.B. (1986). Networks: Between markets and hierarchies. *Strategic Management Journal, 7*(1), 37–51.

Voss, G.B., and Voss, Z.G. (2000). Strategic orientation and firm performance in an artistic environment. *Journal of Marketing, 64*(1), 67–83.

Wang, Q., and Chen, X. (2012). Regulatory transparency: How China can learn from Japan's nuclear regulatory failures? *Renewable and Sustainable Energy Reviews, 16*(6), 3574–3578.

Willianson, P.J., and De Meyer, A. (2012). Ecosystem advantage: How to successfully harness the power of partners. *California Management Review, 55*(1), 24–46.

Zhou, S., and Zhang, X. (2010). Nuclear energy development in China: A study of opportunities and challenges. *Energy, 35*(11), 4282–4288.

Zhou, Y., Rengifo, C., Chen, P., and Hinze, J. (2011). Is China ready for its nuclear expansion? *Energy Policy, 39*(2), 771–781.

7. Revisiting SOEs' innovation in the large infrastructure sector

From the seemingly correct argument that state-owned enterprises (SOEs) lack incentives to innovate due to monopoly (Tan, 2001), to the irrefutable facts that some of the Chinese SOEs made remarkable innovation achievements, we assume the debates on whether SOEs can innovate will go on. Nevertheless, the ecosystem-based and user-driven collaborations seem to continue playing a critical role in large-scale infrastructure innovation projects led by SOEs. The entrepreneurial Chinese government will still significantly drive SOEs to develop cutting-edge technologies in the future. Based on the stories shared in previous chapters, we try to summarize the determinants of Chinese SOEs' innovation in large infrastructure sector, and discuss the advantages and disadvantages of China's unique innovation model.

7.1   DOMESTIC MARKET DEMAND AND SCALE

With the largest population and the third-largest territory all over the world, China has an extraordinarily huge market scale. Many studies have already mentioned that market is as important as technology in driving innovation. As Chinese companies are still lagging behind in certain technological areas, how to utilize and leverage the potential of the domestic market to gain competitive advantage is a fundamental issue for large SOEs.

Another important matter for SOEs is how to sense and take advantage of the dynamically changing windows of opportunity. Together with the fast economic and social development of China in the past several decades, the market demand has evolved from basic consumer goods to diversified and advanced goods. Together with the continuous upgrade, the demands on basic supplies, such as more efficient electric power, quicker passenger and cargo transport over long distance, and faster multifunctional mobile telecommunications, have kept on increasing on an even larger scale. This also stimulates the international giants in relevant industries, such as high-speed rail, telecommunications, and nuclear power, to resolutely enter the Chinese market for a share.

However, due to China's distinctive contexts, it is unavoidable that the foreign advanced technology has to be localized and further innovated to satisfy the large-scale and divergent market demands of China. This, however, can be better realized by the SOEs which profoundly understand Chinese situations and have considerable resource advantages, especially in the industries requiring extensive economies of scale and large amounts of research and development (R&D) input.

Figure 7.1 implies that from 2006 to 2016, electricity generation and consumption in China were increasing in step, at a high rate. The volume in 2016 was approximately 6 trillion kWh, double that in 2006. This implies that the huge domestic demand for electric power will keep increasing with the country's fast development. Similarly, from 2004 to 2014, the national railway's passenger delivery volume increased from 10 to 24 billion people (Figure 7.2), with an average annual growth rate of 8.98 percent. From 2013 to 2018, the mobile Internet access dataflow drastically swelled from 12.7 to 711 billion GB, and the dataflow of usage increased from 0.13 to 4.42 GB/month/ household (Figure 7.3). Nevertheless, these numbers do not imply a saturated market; with China's fast development and urbanization, huge volumes of new market demands will be stimulated.

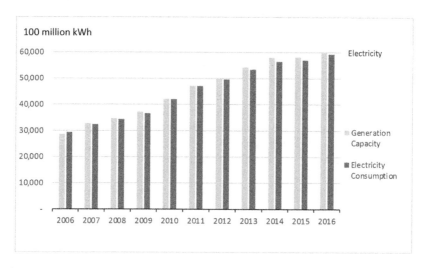

Figure 7.1   *Electricity generation and consumption from 2006 to 2016 in China*

All the cases discussed earlier in this book – high-speed rail, 4G telecommunications, ultra-high voltage power transmission, and nuclear power plant – were backed up by the huge-scale and dynamic domestic market demands. Moreover, all the markets are nascent ones that are not fully competitive, which could be somehow manipulated and influenced by those large SOEs

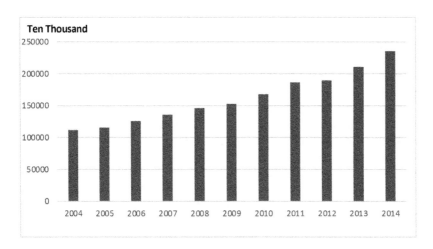

Figure 7.2   National railway passenger delivery volume in China from 2004 to 2014

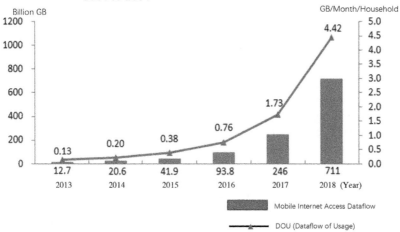

Figure 7.3   China Mobile Internet access dataflow and monthly DOU growth from 2013 to 2018

and the government. This can explain why large SOEs in other sectors (for example, automobile and integrated circuit) cannot compete with private enterprises or multinationals, even with similar governmental supports.

7.2   GOVERNMENTAL DEMANDS AND SUPPORTS

According to the previous chapters, the SOEs under direct supervision of the State Asset Supervision and Administration Committee (SASAC) have successfully established innovation ecosystems that incorporate all components of their full industrial chains. However, without the substantial governmental supports, the SOEs' innovation ecosystems may hardly come into existence. As elaborated in the first chapter, most SOEs were less competitive in the market in terms of their technological innovations and managerial capabilities. Market demand was not sufficiently powerful to drive the unprepared SOEs to innovate for meeting the demand, as happened commonly in well-developed market economies. Hence, additional forces were needed. The cases shared in this book put forward a clear message that demands from an institutional actor such as the government play an essential role in urging SOEs' initiatives on technological innovation, enhancing the effects of large-scale and urgent market demands (for example, high-speed passenger transport), and catalyzing the formation and sustainability of innovation ecosystems.

Yet people may be confused by the phrase "the demands of the government." With the legacy of the planned economy, China is a middle-income socialist country in the catching-up stage. It becomes crucial to deploy technological development and innovations to transform the "world factory" into a high-income state. For national security as well as international power and influence, China will have to attach importance to the development of strategic technologies to realize a smart catch-up.

In the four areas of large infrastructure sector discussed in this book, all have attracted national interests. Thus it is not only an issue of technological upgrading or satisfying market demands; political concerns are also involved (Breznitz and Murphree, 2011). For the Chinese government, the major demand is to cross the middle-income phase as soon as possible, based on the development of momentous technologies, innovation ecosystems, and industrial clusters (Cai, 2012). For example, from 2005 to 2014, the number of governmental policies for promoting technological innovations, especially the number of jointly issued policies by several governmental departments from 2011, showed an upward trend, implying increasing concerns on technological innovation among separate governmental departments and governmental authorities on different levels (Figure 7.4). Besides, more effective and efficient environmental protection, reducing consumption of strategic resources such as arable land, as well as more comprehensive social development are also comprehensive governmental pursuits (Chen, 2018).

Urging the SOEs to cope with the market demand by virtue of the whole-nation system is relatively easy for the government, while effectively

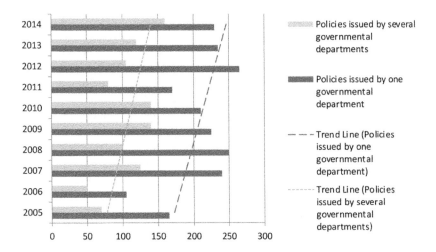

Figure 7.4   *The number of innovation policies issued by the Chinese government from 2005 to 2014*

incentivizing SOEs to develop technologies sustainably and reach a global leading position can be quite difficult. Without appropriate innovation eco-systems enabling resource sharing and value co-creation among innovation partners, the SOEs themselves can hardly satisfy the aforementioned governmental comprehensive needs. To catalyze the segmented resources and actors to constitute an ecosystem, the Chinese government, under these circumstances, entrepreneurially and strategically played a critical role with the help of the whole-nation system. The Chinese government first identified opportunities based on the huge unmet domestic demands with strategic importance to national development. Then the government stimulated SOEs to engage in technological innovation in the strategic areas, and enacted supportive industrial policies. Third, with the jointly developed technical standard systems (with the SOEs and research institutions), the government expedited formation of the SOEs' innovation ecosystems and collaborative innovations among the actors. Consequently, with the governmental guide and support, the SOEs' technological innovation and management are greatly improved to cope with global competition and to continuously create value in domestic and overseas markets.

Take the high-speed rail technology as an example. Although there had been substantial market demand, simply importing foreign products and technologies to meet the huge domestic demand would be extremely costly. Moreover, completely relying on the foreign technologies could hardly meet the domestic demand, due to the particularly divergent geographic and geologic situations in China (see Chapter 5). Thus the complexity of the domestic market induced further technical development. To address those domestic market requirements with technological innovations, decrease dependence on foreign technology, and increase national wealth sustainably, the Chinese government mobilized considerable resources with the whole-nation system to thoroughly learn, absorb, and localize the foreign technology. The measure adopted by the Chinese government is also a common practice for other latecomers. Furthermore, realizing high-speed rail's strategic implications of upgrading domestic infrastructure and developing generic technologies, the "Beijing Model" was constantly employed by the government (Lee, 2013). The model can be illustrated as follows: obtain foreign technology with Chinese market potential, and facilitate domestic enterprises' quick learning and R&D for upgrading the obtained technology, so as to decrease the patent royalty and dependence on foreign technologies, and to realize the advancement and differentiation of domestic technologies and products. Nevertheless, most Chinese domestic companies did not have sufficient R&D capabilities back then, and R&D for advanced and complex technologies usually imply higher levels of uncertainties and risks. Thus Chinese government authorities such as the (former) Ministry of Railways and Ministry of Science and Technology provided funding support through various public subsidy programs.

According to prior studies (e.g., Breznitz and Murphree, 2011), the newly industrialized countries usually subsidize enterprises in the promoted industries to lower their costs for innovation activities. However, this approach does not work effectively if there is no compatible ecosystem formed and no industrial standard system developed. Essentially, whether government support will lead to failure (Breznitz and Murphree, 2011) largely depends on the approach adopted by the government. Drawing on the experiences of other countries, the Chinese government did not simply protect the SOEs with subsidies. Rather, the government deployed a facilitating approach to formulate advanced technical standard systems: they not only regulated the outcomes of the technologies desired, but also were conducive to innovation ecosystems' formation, since all the relevant enterprises had to collaborate to achieve those technical standards. The need for innovation ecosystem was thus strengthened, especially when the technological area and standard system were in accordance with national strategic concerns, such as developing generic technologies and comprehensive industrial clusters for technological leadership. This is not just a balance between protecting SOEs and stimulating their efficiency (Zhou et al., 2017): essentially this is an advanced approach to expedite SOEs' growth for technological competitiveness.

Besides the strategic implications of the high-speed rail projects for technological leadership, advanced industrial clusters, and national wealth, those projects can help to meet other important governmental demands such as saving arable areas (rail electric multiple units, or EMUs, can run on viaducts above land), protecting the environment (EMUs use electricity as the power source), and comprehensive social development (with EMUs, population mobility, urbanization, and de-centralization can be facilitated). Therefore, developing the high-speed train technology was fully supported by the government. With the whole-nation system's advantages, the Chinese government efficiently mobilized considerable resources for the China South Locomotive & Rolling Stock Co., Ltd (CSR) to learn the foreign technologies on the one hand; while on the other hand, besides huge financial supports, as the institutional end-user (back then, the Ministry of Railways was operating the passenger and cargo transport), with industrial policies and regulations the government requested and initiated developing the technical standard systems jointly with the firms and research institutions. This greatly facilitated the formation and upgrading of the ecosystem as all the relevant but internationally less competent domestic enterprises had to align their efforts to innovate in order to meet all the criteria of those technical standard systems, which in turn expedited the success of Chinese high-speed rail technology within a remarkably short period. Similarly, developing the technical standard systems of the ultra-high voltage power transmission, advanced mobile telecommunications, and nuclear power plants was greatly supported by the government as those technologies also meet the aforementioned governmental demand for comprehensive development. Strong governmental support paved the way for the rapid successes of radical innovation in those infrastructure projects.

7.3 STATE-OWNED ENTERPRISES' CAPABILITIES AND ACTIONS

Conventionally, SOEs were regarded as impediments to technological innovations (Zhou et al., 2017). From the perspective of monopoly, SOEs do not have the motives to conduct innovation activities, especially the advanced technological innovations that are highly costly and risky. Nevertheless, as China is becoming increasingly open and advocating worldwide free trade, the monopolies of SOEs are being threatened by both domestic and foreign competitors. For example, in the infrastructure industries such as transport and telecommunications, private enterprises and foreign actors are very active in terms of technological innovation in the Chinese market. Moreover, the Chinese government has the ultimate demand of comprehensive development in economic, social, and environmental dimensions. As vital implementers of the governmental economic strategies, SOEs are required to help meet the governmental requirements (see Chapter 1). Thus with huge domestic market potential, increasing threats of international competitors, as well as the governmental demands and supportive actions, SOEs are spurred to develop their innovation capabilities through: engaging in international competition, spotting the "windows of opportunity" (Lee, 2013) to realize technological leadership and thus economic returns.

The experiences of South Korea indicate that enterprises in newly industrialized countries should not simply follow the mature technologies from developed countries. Rather, the latecomers should take the opportunities of technological paradigm change, use quick iterations to decrease dependence on the mature technologies, and further develop new ones. Moreover, for the catching-up enterprises, entering the emerging areas is a key strategy, since those areas are new to both the dominant and late-developing enterprises (Lee, 2013), such as the high-speed train with a running speed over 350 km/h, ultra-high voltage (UHV) power transmission, and 4G/5G mobile telecommunications. For the innovation projects in industries with existing foreign advanced technology, the SOEs chose to collaborate with their international partners to build solid technical foundations for subsequent iterations on the one hand, and to mobilize their abundant resources to develop new technologies based on the knowledge learnt to better meet Chinese market demands on the other hand. If there is no such foreign advanced technology to learn, independent R&D will have to be the only option, such as the UHV power transmission project led by State Grid.

In those infrastructure industries, the Chinese SOEs actually have considerable advantages in developing new technologies due to their possession of relevant resources (for example, the laboratories and research institutes as well as numerous affiliated firms with different expertise along the entire industrial chains), and the large-scale financial input that they can utilize. Notwithstanding, only relying on the resource advantages cannot guarantee the success of building technological advantages. To realize technological leadership, SOEs will have to put much more effort into developing technical standard systems and innovation ecosystems based on their resource advantages, since the former largely determine the starting points and directions of technological development, while the latter principally facilitate sustainable advancement of the technologies.

It turns out that the technologies developed for a large-scale and multi-demand market such as China will be extraordinarily competitive for meeting market demands in other countries, especially in the high-tech industries such as high-speed rail and mobile telecommunications. From the perspective of reverse innovation (e.g., Govindarajan and Ramamurti, 2011; Shan and Khan, 2016), the SOEs can yield disruptive innovations for developed markets (originally for emerging markets); from the perspective of market potential, making excess profit can be facilitated since those technologies have great value in global markets (not only for developed markets). This further implies that once the technologies are needed in international markets, such as the high-speed train, UHV power transmission, and 4G and 5G mobile telecommunications, more collaborations with international players can be anticipated. International collaborative innovation is not only for market expansion, but also for further technological co-development to meet divergent evolving demands. Probably the accumulated capabilities of SOEs in facilitating and leveraging innovation ecosystems to develop technologies, products, and services jointly with domestic and international partners can also be generalized and improved in subsequent international scenarios.

7.4   RESEARCH INSTITUTIONS AND UNIVERSITIES

It is well acknowledged that in most major innovation achievements, universities and research institutions play a quite important role, especially in the early stage of an innovation process where basic research and scientific exploration for subsequent technological development are essential. In fact, research institutions can be seen as key suppliers of creativity as well as origins of new technologies.

In China, as mentioned in Chapter 2, a few government-led research institutions and national laboratories transformed into technology-based enterprises in the late 1990s. These institutes now have dual identities as enterprises and research forces, and need to balance the logics of profit-seeking and scientific and technological knowledge-seeking. In fact, some succeeded in converting the contradictory roles into synergies. They actively participate in the development of industries with strategic significance to China, and most of them maintain their leading upstream position in the industries, and collaborate closely with SOEs to further transform their scientific and technological knowledge.

According to Keun Lee (2013), Chinese research institutions were greatly conducive to the success of Chinese technological innovation due to their key roles in promoting forward engineering instead of backward engineering; the former basically implies further exploration of new technological paradigms based on current ones, whereas the latter largely relates to gradual improvement of current technologies. However, Chinese research institutions have not always been in a pioneering position. They started from a comparatively backward position, and they learn and evolve with their clients (firms and government), and try to improve their R&D capabilities, aiming to be globally competitive.

The core competences of any research institution in the world obviously reside in their research capabilities, relevant facilities and equipment, as well as research outcomes. Yet without leading-edge research projects and subjects, the capabilities cannot be developed, the facilities and equipment cannot be granted, and the outcomes cannot be generated. Thus for most

Chinese research institutions, just like those in developed countries, obtaining opportunities for leading-edge research with abundant funding is one of their key demands. Since Chinese domestic firms' development was usually not innovation-driven back then, the chances of research institutions participating in pertinent projects were rare. Nevertheless, to fulfill the comprehensive development demand, the Chinese government provided substantial supports in major infrastructure innovation projects such as UHV (power transmission), high-speed rail, LTE-TDD (4G mobile telecommunications), and nuclear power. Hence, the research institutions came to seize the opportunities because of those projects' implications for significantly improving the research institutions' academic competences. Besides, with the whole-nation system's powerful support, the research institutions were called upon to participate in those mega-projects with their dedication to the momentous technological achievements for the country (see Chapter 1). This explains why the collaborations between the SOEs and Chinese research institutions (for example, Chinese Academy of Sciences) as well as public universities were initially promoted by the government, the research institutions and universities became quite actively involved in those projects later on (see Chapter 5). The opportunities and funding for leading-edge research and technology development substantially helped the Chinese research institutions and public universities to attain their global academic impacts by patent applications and research publications.

It can be anticipated that, with the development of the leading-edge technologies, the Chinese research institutions and public universities will be more and more actively engaged in relevant basic research for groundbreaking technologies. The whole-nation system will continuously support and encourage them to dedicate their resources and efforts to the collaborative projects which are strategically critical for Chinese technological and economic development. In the future, with the substantial progress in research competitiveness, it can be anticipated that Chinese leading research intuitions and universities will contribute substantially not only to domestic radical or disruptive innovations, but also to international collaborative projects.

7.5   GOVERNMENT OFFICIALS AS ENTREPRENEURS?

Innovation in the large infrastructure sector likely causes profound impacts on people's daily lives and the economic and social development. Meanwhile, the large infrastructure innovation projects are also associated with higher levels of risk and uncertainty, which require an entrepreneurial spirit and dedication. According to our observation and analysis, the leading personnel such as chief executive officers (CEOs) and chairmen in the cases included in this book exhibited substantial entrepreneurship, but in a different way compared to that of private business entrepreneurs.

Liu Zhenya, a key engineer for State Grid, is the former board chairman of State Grid and the core figure of the UHV project. He graduated from Shandong Institute of Technology majoring in Electrical Engineering and worked on the front line for 21 years. Based on his work experience, he identified several issues related to the power sector: the shortage of power supply with the economic development of China, the geographically unmatched power resources and consumption, and the side effects and low cost efficiency of coal transportation for power generation. He believed that in the next decades, China would need much more electric power for its economic growth, and it would be a mission for the electric power engineers to help address the issue. He foresaw that the voltage level and transmission capacity of power grids would inevitably rise with the increase in power consumption, and firmly insisted that the UHV technology had to be the ultimate solution. He emphasized that developing the UHV technology is not only for China's extra-long-distance power transmission, but also for environmental protection in the long run, as fewer power plants such as coal and hydro will be established due to the UHV technology. Thus he initiated pilot R&D in 2004 and finished the test line when he became the CEO of State Grid, where he developed his idea that the power grid should function like the highway network to facilitate resource flow and allocation.

With the skeptics from the corporation, industry and media, Liu Zhenya insisted on the idea that the UHV project can significantly solve the problem by more efficiently transmitting electric power from West China, which has abundant power resources, to East China, which needs a much greater power supply, despite this implying a large budget for its development. He mobilized all the relevant resources of research and construction for maturing this technology and closely monitored the progress. In 2006, Liu delivered a keynote speech at the International Conference on UHV International Transmission Technology, systematically expounded his vision of an integrated national grid based on UHV, and officially announced that China was about to enter the "UHV era." In 2009, the commercial operation of UHV was launched. After 2013, under the background of air pollution control across China, Liu proposed more UHV lines to help decrease coal power generation in East China. By 2016, seven UHV construction projects had been finished, and 11 projects were works-in-progress. Though he retired in 2016, as his legacy, his vision of interconnecting the grids across the world to better mobilize and allocate global electric power will become a long-term strategy of State Grid.

Liu Zhijun, the former minister of the (former) Ministry of Railways, was the core figure of the high-speed rail project. He graduated from Southwest Jiaotong University, majoring in Transportation Management, and had accumulated rich experience from working at the grass-roots level. Learning from the Japanese Shinkansen, he gradually realized that high-speed rail would be the future of China's rail transportation, and it could significantly help to increase the transportation capacity of China's rail system, and stimulate economic growth along the high-speed lines. However, back then, China did not have the capacity to produce such trains, while only a few international giants could do so. More importantly, simply purchasing from international giants was not viable, as the quoted price was far beyond an affordable budget. Thus, Liu Zhijun invited the major international manufacturers' representatives to Beijing, and negotiated with them one by one to lower the price offer. With the lure of China's huge market, and to gain a larger share of the pie, the representatives revealed the defects of their competitors' products, and the price offers were thereby lowered substantially.

However, Liu knew that only purchasing the finished products could not be an effective option for the sustainable development of China's high-speed rail technology. Thus he negotiated for importing the relevant technologies as well, and eventually succeeded. Then he started the next strategy for technology learning, absorbing, and innovating, and correspondingly mobilized relevant domestic resources including all the key manufacturers, research institutes, and universities to upgrade the learnt technology. Actually, he was also criticized by stakeholders mainly because of the extraordinarily high price of developing high-speed rail, involving purchasing finished products and technologies, as well as constructing the specialized tracks. Nevertheless, he managed to proceed by putting forward the high-speed train project as the solution to the large-volume transportation pressure during important domestic festivals and holidays. By virtue of the Chinese government's rescue plan after the financial crisis in 2008, Liu managed to acquire huge financial support (1.5 trillion CNY) for the high-speed rail project. With the operation of several pilot lines, the necessity for and superior performance of high-speed rail were well recognized by society. Besides, with his vision of maintaining high running speed, a large number of viaducts and tunnels were adopted, which in turn greatly helped to improve the construction capabilities of Chinese companies. Though Liu eventually was sentenced to prison due to corruption, his entrepreneurship as well as his strategic vision and decisions played a key role at the pilot stage of China's high-speed rail development.

Xi Guohua, the core figure promoting the development of LTE-TDD, graduated from Hefei University of Technology majoring in electrical automation, and worked as a laboratory technician for six years before he was appointed to a deputy management position in the (former) Administrative Bureau of Post and Telecommunications Shanghai. After the appointment, he had opportunities to receive advanced training in Italy and the United States (for example, senior management training with AT&T). He came to realize the strategic implications of telecommunications for economic growth as basic facilities. With his promotions, he had more and more opportunities to understand telecommunications development in China, and formed a clearer idea about the future of this industry. The unsuccessful development of China Mobile's 3G concerned him and he realized the importance of technological compatibility and leadership. After becoming the Vice-Minister of Industry and Information Technology, he was quite concerned about the development of LTE-TDD, and when he took up position as the board chairman of China Mobile, more efforts were put into it for the key opportunity of 4G licensing by the Ministry of Industry and Information Technology. Based on his work experience and reflection, he knew the importance of technological leadership, but also attached importance to international collaboration for technological compatibility. After being licensed by the Ministry of Industry and Information Technology, with a large number of base stations allocated domestically and abroad, LTE-TDD was widely adopted. Although Xi retired, his judgment of the shortened period of technological advance in telecommunications industry, and his vision for 5G, significantly promoted the collaborative technology development of China Mobile.

Obviously, the important leaders of the major innovation achievements shared in this book exhibited remarkable entrepreneurial spirit, strategic thinking, and capability in adopting effectual tactical approaches. With strong patriotism and relevant engineering backgrounds, as well as abundant front-line work experience, they knew the technological bottlenecks and details well, and had the capability to capture the breakthrough points and mobilize resources towards the promising directions of technological evolution. That is how these entrepreneurs leveraged the whole-nation system's strength with their vision and influence.

When talking about entrepreneurship, people usually focus on the individual-level phenomena. For those large infrastructure innovation projects shared in this book, corporate and governmental entrepreneurship also played a quite substantial role besides the individual-level one.

With evolution of the SOEs' technological and managerial capabilities, they can be more and more experienced in identifying key business opportunities and mobilizing resources for subsequent exploitation with innovations, such as 5G and Maglev. Furthermore, as well as domestic achievements, Chinese SOEs are actively engaged in developing overseas markets, and these international initiatives and experiences will in turn stimulate further corporate entrepreneurship.

The rejuvenation of Japan and the rise of South Korea show that governmental officials can act as entrepreneurs (Link, 2010; Link and Link, 2009; Link and Scott, 2010) and play a proactive role in helping their domestic enterprises to grow through mobilizing divergent resources. Basically, the governmental entrepreneurship allows the Chinese government to identify and exploit the key opportunities to meet its comprehensive national needs by mobilizing the nationwide resources. The particularity of governmental entrepreneurship, compared to corporate and individual entrepreneurship, is that it is more related to identifying and exploiting the opportunities crucial for the entire country's long-term development. Thus the risk level, scale, coverage, and profoundness of governmental entrepreneurship are far different from those of corporate or individual entrepreneurship. However, all the three types of entrepreneurship actually interplayed with each other, jointly spurring the SOEs' R&D, innovation ecosystems' evolution, and technological breakthroughs.

7.6   SOES' INNOVATION AND THE CHINA MODEL

Overall, the Chinese SOEs' radical innovations in mega infrastructure projects were triggered by various demands at different stages, supported by the whole-nation system led by the government, driven by diverse entrepreneurship (including governmental and corporate entrepreneurship), and gradually realized and advanced by the formation and development of innovation ecosystems.

Breznitz and Murphree (2011) argued that nationalism played an important role in Chinese governmental support for industrial development. In the cases of high-speed rail, UHV power transmission, and nuclear power plant, this argument seemed to be true. However, it was the distinctive national conditions instead of the nationalism that caused the domestic collaborative innovations. For example, the advanced high-speed rail technology suitable for highly complex operating environments, and the UHV power transmission over extremely long distances, were not urgently needed in overseas markets back then, and foreign companies did not have the complete solutions. For nuclear power, due to the huge territory and populations of China as well as its fast development, the shortage of power supply became an increasingly serious issue. Nevertheless, purely importing foreign final products or technologies would be quite expensive due to the increasingly large scale of demands and constant technological upgrades. Developing those technologies thus had to depend on domestic collaborative innovation. Comparatively, the 4G mobile telecommunications was a universally needed technology and it did not depend on specific contexts so heavily; thus collaborating with international partners, rather than merely domestic partners (in the development of 3G), was a better option. We believe that with the increase of international demand for Chinese technologies, collaborating with international partners will become more and more common, and the pertinent innovation ecosystems will be expanded internationally.

The international product life cycle (IPLC) theory suggests that the newly industrialized countries should just follow the development process of the mature industries in developed countries (Lee, 2013). However, with the emergence of new technologies and continuous technological development, the mature technologies controlled by developed countries may be outdated and less competitive in the changing global market. That is to say, the newly industrialized countries will have equal opportunities compared with developed countries when new windows of opportunity open. The successes of East Asian countries such as Japan and South Korea are good examples, and the Chinese SOEs' innovations further challenge the IPLC approach. It seems that the Chinese SOEs can and will innovate, which will be proved by more and more remarkable technological achievements in the future. Furthering the Beijing Mode suggested by Keun Lee (2013), we argue that technology import or development based on multi-demand, quick learning, and iteration with upgraded or new technical standard systems, as well as collaborative R&D and open innovation ecosystems, might be a common process of Chinese SOEs' innovation in the next decades.

In developed countries, market and governmental activities are regarded as paradoxical forces in economic development, and the government should intervene in the market as little as possible (Pigou, 2017). However, the cases shared in this book imply that in developing countries, especially at the industrialization stage, the government can significantly promote economic development not only by building infrastructure, but also by stimulating SOEs' sustainable innovation for upgrading the infrastructure and thus meeting the evolving market demands for public goods.

The Chinese government was rather concerned about the huge-scale unmet domestic market demands in infrastructure industries, due to their immense nationwide impacts. In the relevant projects, the government acted as an entrepreneur, taking more risks to encourage the SOEs to engage in the process of meeting the evolving and huge-scale domestic market demands with technological innovations. It turned out that the SOEs can sustainably innovate by establishing and coordinating their respective innovation ecosystems. Since all of the centrally managed SOEs' businesses are closely related to the large-scale infrastructure sector, the governmental actions have substantially driven the infrastructure's rapid evolution with the SOEs' technological innovations. This in turn paved a broad way for flourishing businesses of all the companies (besides the ecosystems' participants) based on the innovation ecosystems' core technologies and their economic and social impacts, leading to subsequent market prosperity and sustainable economic development. With China's fast development, we can foresee that there will be further huge market demand for public goods based on more advanced technologies such as big data and artificial intelligence, which in turn calls upon the governmental initiatives in incubating more open and international innovation ecosystems.

7.7   HYBRID SOES AND THE CHINA MODEL'S LIMITATIONS

SOEs, compared to private enterprises, on average have more advanced technological bases, but their innovations are more subject to governmental approval. Implied by SOEs' mission of fulfilling governmental requirements (Zhou et al., 2006), the state logic plays the central role in guiding their actions, including safeguarding national security and maintaining the employment rate (Park and Ungson, 2001; Boubakri et al., 2008), as well as ensuring political control especially in strategic sectors such as the military, petroleum, and telecommunications (Greve and Zhang, 2017). Since 2012, under Xi Jinping's new political regime, large SOEs have been required to better support political efforts (for example, the Belt and Road), and the business leaders have been given more political identification. On August 24, 2015, the Guiding Opinions on Deepening the Reform of State-owned Enterprises highlighted that SOEs should be led by the Communist Party of China, and should be more competitive and prosperous to facilitate China's economic development.

Meanwhile, market logic is compatible with the state logic when SOEs try to achieve core goals such as increasing their financial performance (Greve and Zhang, 2017). Since 2004, SASAC and the Ministry of Finance have issued several policies to stimulate SOEs' value maintenance and increase (SASAC, 2004; MOF, 2007). Furthermore, the call for indigenous innovation implied the requirement of increasing SOEs' R&D input to grow their assets' value (SASAC, 2009). Accordingly, from 2006 to 2009, SOEs increased their R&D investment by an average annual rate of 28.5 percent, and the R&D inputs accounted for 2.1 percent of their revenue by 2009.[1]

Essentially, all the SOEs' radical innovation projects discussed in this book have positive externalities and spillovers, and thus are supported by the entire society in spite of their questionable financial returns. For example, although the high-speed rail is socially successful, its economic return is still far from what was anticipated. Due to the first goal of ensuring national security and social stability based on the state logic (Frye and Shleifer, 1997; Nee, 1992), they primarily focus on neither profitability (Peng and Delios, 2006) nor effi-

---

[1]   The central government's investment in science and technology (S&T) increased by 28.5 percent annually during the Eleventh Five-Year Plan period, http://cn.chinagate .cn/enterprises/2011-02/22/content_21974774.htm (in Chinese)

ciency (Wong et al., 2004). In this sense, innovations in the large infrastructure sector seem to be tailored for large Chinese SOEs.

By contrast, SOEs seem to be not so innovative in highly dynamic industries with intense rivalry. For example, in the information and communication technology (ICT) industries, SOEs do not earn their footholds, and in China we can only see dominance of the giants such as Alibaba and Tencent. This, again, is related to SOEs' hybrid character. SOEs cannot make strategic decisions rapidly or incentivize employees flexibly as PEs do, due to the strict control or intervention by various supervisory authorities. Hence, the aforementioned China Model of innovation only works in the sectors or areas with explicit market demands and technological directions as well as SOEs' dominance.

In fact, SOEs are more capable of technological catch-up and indigenous innovation in the large infrastructure sector; nonetheless, once the country has no more such infrastructure projects to be launched, it will be quite challenging for the large SOEs to survive. Maybe exploring international markets and upgrading or building newly needed infrastructure will eventually become the alternatives for their survival and tenable radical innovations. But owing to their hybrid nature, as well as insufficient market-oriented operation and modern business management, there can be far more challenges for Chinese SOEs to sustainably develop, and thus further chances for the China Model to evolve.

REFERENCES

Boubakri, N., Cosset, J.-C., and Saffar, W. (2008). Political connections of newly privatized firms. *Journal of Corporate Finance, 14*(5), 654–673.
Breznitz, D., and Murphree, M. (2011). *Run of the Red Queen: Government, Innovation, Globalization, and Economic Growth in China.* New Haven, CT: Yale University Press.
Cai, F. (2012). Is there a "middle-income trap"? Theories, experiences and relevance to China. *China and World Economy, 20*(1), 49–61.
Chen, S. (2018). *Energy, Environment and Economic Transformation in China.* London, UK and New York, USA: Routledge.
Frye, T., and Shleifer, A. (1997). The invisible hand and the grabbing hand. *American Economic Review, 87*, 354–358.
Govindarajan, V., and Ramamurti, R. (2011). Reverse innovation, emerging markets, and global strategy. *Global Strategy Journal, 1*(3–4), 191–205.
Greve, H.R., and Zhang, C.M. (2017). Institutional logics and power sources: Merger and acquisition decisions. *Academy of Management Journal, 60*(2), 671–694.
Lee, K. (2013). *Schumpeterian Analysis of Economic Catch-up: Knowledge, Path-Creation, and the Middle-Income Trap.* Cambridge: Cambridge University Press.
Link, A.N. (2010). Government as entrepreneur: Reframing a dimension of science and technology policy. *Research Policy, 39*(5), 565–566.

Link, A.N., and Link, J.R. (2009). *Government as Entrepreneur*. Oxford: Oxford University Press.

Link, A.N., and Scott, J.T. (2010). Government as entrepreneur: Evaluating the commercialization success of SBIR projects. *Research Policy*, *39*(5), 589–601.

MOF (2007). Interim measures for confirming the value maintenance and appreciation of the state-owned assets of financial enterprises (in Chinese). Retrieved from: http://www.mof.gov.cn/zhengwuxinxi/caizhengxinwen/200805/t20080519_24996.htm.

Nee, V. (1992). Organizational dynamics of market transition: Hybrid forms, property rights, and mixed economy in China. *Administrative Science Quarterly*, *37*, 1–27.

Park, S.H., and Ungson, G.R. (2001). Interfirm rivalry and managerial complexity: A conceptual framework of alliance failure. *Organization Science*, *12*(1), 37–53.

Peng, M.W., and Delios, A. (2006). What determines the scope of the firm over time and around the world? An Asia Pacific perspective. *Asia Pacific Journal Management*, *23*, 385–405.

Pigou, A. (2017). *The Economics of Welfare*. London, UK and New York, USA: Routledge.

SASAC (2004). Interim measures for confirming the value maintenance and appreciation of the state-owned assets of enterprises (in Chinese). Retrieved from: http://www.sasac.gov.cn/n2588035/n2588320/n2588335/c4259593/content.html.

SASAC (2009). Interim measures for assessing the operating performance of the persons in charge of the centrally managed enterprises (in Chinese). Retrieved from: http://old.sasac.gov.cn/n2588035/n2588320/n2588335/c4259003/content.html.

Shan, J., and Khan, M.A. (2016). Implications of reverse innovation for socio-economic sustainability: A case study of Philips China. *Sustainability*, *8*(6), 530.

Tan, J. (2001). Innovation and risk-taking in a transitional economy: A comparative study of Chinese managers and entrepreneurs. *Journal of Business Venturing*, *16*(4), 359–376.

Wong, S.M., Opper, S., and Hu, R. (2004). Shareholding structure, depoliticization and firm performance. *Economics of Transition*, *12*(1), 29–66.

Zhou, K.Z., David, K.T., and Li, J.J. (2006). Organizational changes in emerging economies: Drivers and consequences. *Journal of International Business Studies*, *37*(2), 248–263.

Zhou, K.Z., Gao, G.Y., and Zhao, H. (2017). State ownership and firm innovation in China: An integrated view of institutional and efficiency logics. *Administrative Science Quarterly*, *62*(2), 375–404.

Index